IRAQ—
BABYLON OF THE END-TIMES?

IRAQ—
BABYLON OF THE END-TIMES?

C. Marvin Pate

and

J. Daniel Hays

 Baker Books

A Division of Baker Book House Co
Grand Rapids, Michigan 49516

© 2003 by C. Marvin Pate and J. Daniel Hays

Published by Baker Books
a division of Baker Book House Company
P.O. Box 6287, Grand Rapids, MI 49516-6287
www.bakerbooks.com

Second printing, April 2003

Printed in the United States of America

Library of Congress Cataloging-in-Publication Data is on file at the Library of Congress, Washington, D.C.

ISBN 0-8010-6479-1

To those who have dedicated their lives
to sharing the gospel with Muslims

Contents

ONE

The Russians Are Out and the Muslims Are In

Marilyn and Bill, a delightful, gracious, middle-aged Christian couple, invited me (Hays) out to lunch after I had preached at their church. We arrived at their favorite restaurant, found a seat, and began chatting casually about various things—football, church, college, and local politics. The waitress brought our food, and as Marilyn began to prepare her baked potato, she looked at me intently, leaned over slightly, and suddenly asked seriously, "Do you know anything about biblical prophecy?"

I was startled by her abrupt and intense manner, and I was unsure how to answer. I regularly teach Old Testament Prophets at a university, we translate a large chunk of Jeremiah in my second-year Hebrew class, and I have written a few things on prophecy, so I was forced to confess, "Well, yes, I know a little."

She nodded. I couldn't tell if her nodding was in approval or disapproval. She piled sour cream on her potato and then looked up again. "I have been reading a fascinating new book by Hal Lindsey," she continued. "He writes in this book that it is not the Russians who will invade Israel in the end-times but rather the Muslims.[1] That is really scary. Look at what the Muslims are trying to do to us. Look at what happened on 9-11. It is pretty clear that we are entering the end-times, don't you think?"

She didn't really seem to be waiting for an answer. She had finished the ritual preparation of her potato and was beginning to enjoy the fruit of her labors. I was wondering how I should answer her. I found myself reminiscing. Back in the seventies, Lindsey had convinced us that the Russians were about to invade Israel. I remember as a college freshman reading his claim that we were entering the end-times in 1971. I pondered asking Marilyn if perhaps Lindsey should apologize for misleading us on this issue thirty years ago before he had switched interpretations. While I hesitated, she looked up again and said, "I do love biblical prophecy. You should study it." She apparently loved baked potatoes as well, for she immediately turned her attention to the spud on her plate, apparently assuming that I didn't really have anything to say on the matter.[2]

Gold Fillings and Underwear

It is undeniably true. American Christians love biblical prophecy every bit as much as they love baked potatoes. Consider the following summary of the opening events of one of America's favorite prophecy books:

10

Rayford Steele, a commercial pilot, was flying over the Atlantic Ocean on a Chicago to London run. For the moment, his only distressing thought was whether or not he should pursue a romantic relationship with the stewardess on board his present flight, but without jeopardizing his already troubled marriage. And, as far as Rayford was concerned, his wife's recent near fanatical attachment to Christianity was not helping the situation. Suddenly, that same stewardess came hurriedly into the cockpit and announced with alarm to the captain that many of the passengers were gone! They had apparently vanished into thin air, leaving only the gold fillings in their teeth and their underwear![3]

Thus begins the blockbuster book series Left Behind. The writers of the Left Behind series then proceed for several volumes to dramatize with utmost sincerity the unfolding of end-time events as foretold in biblical prophecy: the rapture, the Antichrist and the great tribulation, persecution of the Jews and new Christians, Armageddon, and, before the story is over, the second coming of Christ and the millennium. This series has sold over fifty million copies. Indeed, for the past thirty to thirty-five years, Americans have demonstrated a strong fascination with books about the end-times, especially books that connect the current events of our day to biblical prophecy regarding the end.

The roots of this biblical prophecy popularity can probably be traced to the creation of the modern state of Israel in 1948. For the first time in nearly two thousand years, there was a literal country of Israel, and because of the tense politics of the Cold War, the events occurring in Jerusalem were at the center of world attention. By 1967, the explosive events in the Middle East could have easily erupted into worldwide nuclear war. Interpretations of biblical prophecy regarding Israel and the end-times that had long been assumed to be allegorical or symbolic were now reassessed, and a literal interpretation started to seem more and more plausible. Hal Lindsey pulled all these strands together in 1970 with the publication of *The Late Great Planet Earth.* In a stroke of sheer literary genius, Lindsey took the discussion of end-time prophecy out of the hands of scholars and placed it into the hands of everyday Christians. He connected the belief in literal fulfillment of prophecy with the tense events occurring in the Middle East. The foreboding cloud of nuclear war that hung over America in the early seventies made all of us frightened of (and thus very interested in) the possibility of an end-time nuclear holocaust foretold in the Bible. As a college freshman in 1971, I (Hays) brought a copy of *The Late Great Planet Earth* with me to Auburn University. Everyone on my wing of the dormitory, Christian and non-Christian alike, read the book that year. It scared us to death. We thought the end was near.

Does the Bible Say We Are in the End-Times?

Many writers have stressed that the Bible teaches we are near or even in the end-times. The imminence of end-time events is usually deduced from the following passages.

MARK 13:30

In Mark 13:30, Jesus states, "This generation will certainly not pass away until all these things have happened." This prediction refers to the signs of the times immediately preceding Christ's return: wars, famines, false Christs, false prophets, apostasy, and the persecution of Christians. Such signs are usually viewed as the events of the great seven-year tribulation. Certain writers connect these events to current times by underscoring the mention of the budding of fig trees (Mark 13:28–29). They reason that since the fig tree, which decorated the wall of the Jerusalem temple, was a symbol for Israel, the repossession of the land of Israel by the Jews in 1948 began the final generation.[4]

1 THESSALONIANS 4:13–18

But the good news, according to many, is that Scripture passages such as 1 Thessalonians 4:13–18 forecast the snatching away of the church before the great tribulation. This event is known as the rapture. Such a teaching was developed by the Irish (former) Anglican priest John N. Darby in the nineteenth century and was then popularized in the early twentieth century by the Scoffield Bible. This line of thinking is known as dispensationalism. After the dispensation, or period, of the church is brought to an end by the rapture of Christians to heaven, the dispensation of the great tribulation on earth will begin. Those who combine Mark 13:30 and 1 Thessalonians 4:13–18 predict that, if the last generation began in 1948, at the end of which will be the great tribulation, then the rapture must necessarily occur sometime before that generation has concluded. Time is definitely running out.

DANIEL 2, 7, AND 9:24–27

The typical end-time scenario envisioned by many current writers of end-time prophecy centers on Daniel 2,

7, and 9:24–27. Daniel 2 and Daniel 7 prophesy that five kingdoms will comprise world history from the time of Daniel (550 B.C.) to the end of the world: Babylonia, Medo-Persia, Greece, a revived Roman Empire, and, finally, the messianic kingdom, which will crush and rule over all the earth at the return of Christ. Daniel 9:24–27 offers extended comment on the fourth kingdom of Daniel 2 and 7, the kingdom identified as the revived Roman Empire. Many have argued that the prophecy regarding this kingdom will be fulfilled by the European Common Market (currently called the European Union), which will be led by the Antichrist, a Gentile man who offers a panacea for all political and economic world problems. This individual, who feigns religious conviction, will make a peace pact with Israel at the beginning of the final seven years of the last generation. After three and a half years, however, he will break that alliance, and all hell will break loose as he seeks to destroy Israel and true Christians.

EZEKIEL 38–39

The Antichrist, however, will not be alone in his bid to rule the world. Numerous writers state that Ezekiel 38–39 predicts that a foe to the north of Israel will also have his eye on that land, seeking to invade it. It was once fashionable to claim that the Soviet Union would be the major player in such an end-time attack on Israel. But the dismantling of the Soviet Union has caused at least one notable prophecy buff to change his mind on the matter. As mentioned earlier in this chapter, Hal Lindsey now thinks that Iran and the Muslim world will dominate Russia (now only a minor participant in end-time affairs), controlling it by its interest in the oil industry. Others argue that the foe to the north refers to those central Asian Muslim regions that used to be part of the Soviet Union but are now independent. Charles Dyer argues that the unifying element of these countries is their adherence to Islam and that these former Soviet republics will combine with Turkey, Iran, Libya, and the Sudan to form a Muslim alliance that will invade Israel. Therefore, in terms of the enemy from the north who invades Israel in the last days, according to Dyer, the Russians are out and the Muslims are in.[5]

REVELATION 17–18

Still others see Revelation 17–18 as a central text in understanding the connection between biblical prophecy and Middle East current events. Those two chapters in the Book of Revelation, according to this view, compare the future rebuilt city of Babylon to the harlot who rides the beast of the Antichrist. Thus, according to Dyer for example, the Antichrist is the fourth kingdom of Daniel 2 and 7, but the harlot is the rebuilt city of Babylon, which controls the beast and the world because it controls the oil fields of Saudi Arabia, Kuwait, and Iraq. Thus, it should come as no surprise that Revelation 17–18 is on the verge of being fulfilled as Saddam Hussein continues his bid to rule the Middle East. Saddam is rebuilding the literal city of Babylon in fulfillment of biblical prophecy, indicating with certainty that we are entering the end-times.[6]

Is It All True?

While these prophetic themes have captured the imaginations and steeled the faith of Christians for centuries, today they have heightened significance in light of the volatile nature of current events. The attacks on the World Trade Center and the Pentagon on September 11, 2001, rekindled the fear and feelings of vulnerability that Americans have not experienced since the end of the Cold War. Weapons of mass destruction—nuclear, chemical, and biological—are discussed regularly in the media. We all thought that Saddam Hussein's wings had been clipped in the Gulf War of 1991, but once again Iraq is at center stage of world geopolitical events.

Does the new geopolitical role of Iraq and Babylon coincide with biblical prophecy? Is a restored Babylon inevitable, and does Saddam Hussein's dream to rebuild it indicate that we are moving rapidly into the final days? Should we start cleaning out our old Cold War bomb shelters and dispense with our long-term investment planning? If the end is really upon us, then we need to plan for it.

Yet what if current events do not directly coincide with biblical prophecy? The Soviet Union did not invade Israel back in the seventies. The end was not imminently near in 1971, and people like ourselves who went to college rather than prepared for the end of the world apparently made the right decision. As Christians we believe in biblical prophecy, and we want to be obedient to the Lord, but how do we distinguish correct interpretations of prophecy from incorrect ones? We do not want to be naïve or ignorant regarding the momentous events that are transpiring at the present time, but we do not want to be misled into following incorrect interpretations of Scripture either. Are there criteria by which to evaluate the connections between biblical prophecy and the current events taking place in Iraq and the Middle East?

Criteria for evaluating any interpretation of Scripture and for determining the connections between Scripture and current events do exist. Indeed, the goal of this book is to study such connections and to determine the relationship between Saddam Hussein's literal Iraqi city of Babylon and biblical prophecy. We will take a quick look at Saddam Hussein and his dream to rebuild Babylon. We will explore the wonders of ancient Babylon and discuss its role in the biblical world. The name *Babylon* occurs over two hundred times in the Old Testament prophetic books and in 2 Kings. Several of these crucial texts will be examined. Likewise, we will spend some time exploring other central biblical passages that describe end-time events, especially in the books of Ezekiel, Daniel, and Revelation. We will then return to the recent rise to power of Saddam Hussein and the modern Iraqi state and determine the answer to our central question: Do the current events in Iraq and the Middle East indicate that we are entering the end-times predicted in the Bible?

So as you read this book, keep your Bibles open and leave CNN on. It will be an exciting trip that connects history, biblical prophecy, and current geopolitical events in the Middle East.

TWO

Saddam and the Glory of Babylon

When Saddam Hussein clawed and scratched his way to power in Iraq during the 1970s, he inherited a country that was seriously divided along ethnic and religious lines. He also had traditional enemies on his eastern border (the Iranians) and on his western border (the Turks). In fact, the different people groups that have inhabited the area now called Iraq have been fighting against these two traditional enemies off and on for centuries. In an attempt to build some semblance of national unity among the disparate groups of Iraq, Saddam used the state-controlled media as well as educational institutions to teach and constantly remind the Iraqis about ancient Mesopotamian culture and history. This followed the policy that had been established by Abd al Karim Qasim, the Iraqi leader who had preceded him. The apparent goal of this policy was to create national pride and unity based on ancient Mesopotamian history and culture that would cut across the ethnic and religious divisions that have historically divided the people of Iraq. When he became president in 1979, Saddam accelerated these plans, focusing on the glory of the Neo-Babylonian Empire and its most famous king, Nebuchadnezzar. Fusing the political need for national unity with his own natural bent toward megalomania, Saddam attempted to associate himself with the ancient ruler Nebuchadnezzar, and he began making plans to rebuild a full-scale model of the ancient city of Babylon on the original site. Each brick used was to be stamped with Saddam's name.[1] Archaeological records of the ancient city were consulted, and construction began.

By 1988, construction was well under way, and Iraq sponsored the Second International Babylon Festival to celebrate and inform the world of its progress. One of the Western writers invited was Charles Dyer, and he brought back vivid pictures of the reconstructed model of ancient Babylon. Indeed, this visit appears to have been the major inspiration for his book *The Rise of Babylon: Sign of the End Times*.[2] In 1998, *Newsweek* also described the project.[3] In 2002, Rick MacInnes-Rae of CBC Radio visited the new Babylon and reported on the completed complex, noting, however, that the work was a little shabby and that many of the real treasures of ancient Babylon still lay in foreign museums. MacInnes-Rae also reported that Saddam had constructed one of his monstrous—and controversial—private palaces near the Babylonian complex.[4]

What draws Saddam to ancient Babylon? Why does he want his people to view Iraq as a revived Babylon and himself as the new Nebuchadnezzar? Is this simply the foolish delusion of a madman? Or is there more method to his madness than meets the eye? A brief look at the history of Babylon may help us to understand.

The Cradle of Civilization

The modern country of Iraq encompasses the famous ancient region of the world called Mesopotamia. The word *Mesopotamia* means "between the rivers" and applies roughly to the territory between the Tigris and Euphrates Rivers. This is one of the richest areas of ancient history and culture in the entire world. In fact, many scholars refer to this region as the "cradle of civilization," for it was here that some of the world's earliest civilizations arose. As early as 3000 B.C., in the southernmost region of Mesopotamia (near where the Tigris and Euphrates Rivers flow into the Persian Gulf—or the Arabian Gulf, as the Arabs prefer to call it), the Sumerian civilization was flowering. Villages had been transformed into urban centers, and a sophisticated civilization had sprung up around these cities.

The Sumerians developed writing, and they used it extensively for recording government activities and even mundane business transactions. The clay tablets they used for writing have been well preserved throughout the ages, and during the last one hundred years, archaeologists have recovered more than a quarter million clay tablets inscribed in the Sumerian language. Besides writing and government documentation, many other developments that were critical to the rise of civilization have been attributed to the Sumerians: the city-state, the accumulation of capital, the wheel, the potter's wheel, monumental architecture, the number system based on

21

the number 60 (we still use this for time as well as for geometry, i.e., 60 minutes in an hour, 360° in a circle, etc.), schools, and the cylinder seal.[5]

By 2350 B.C., however, the region of Sumer had been conquered by Sargon, who had established one of the first Mesopotamian empires. With its capital at Akkad, Sargon established Akkadian as the main language of Mesopotamia, a feature that remained characteristic of the region for many centuries. It was during Sargon's reign that the city of Babylon first appears in non-biblical literary documents, but it did not play an important role in his empire, remaining instead a minor provincial city during this time. Saddam Hussein has also identified himself with this ancient Akkadian king, for Sargon was the first real imperialistic ruler of the region now known as Iraq.[6]

The Irony of Saddam and Hammurabi

Soon after Sargon came to power, Amorites (literally, "those from the west") began migrating to southern Mesopotamia and growing in power. They adopted the Akkadian language and the old Sumerian-related culture of the region. By 2000 B.C., they were fairly well entrenched in the region, and under their influence the city of Babylon developed into one of their more powerful and important cities. Thus, the next four hundred years are generally referred to as the Old Babylonian Empire. The most famous king of this era was undoubtedly Hammurabi (many current scholars now refer to him as Hammurapi). The spectacular rise to power of Babylon during this time was due to Hammurabi's extensive diplomatic and military skill.

Although the life of the empire he created was brief, the name he brought to the empire stuck, and for more than one thousand years, the entire southern region of Mesopotamia was generally known as Babylonia. Hammurabi, however, is perhaps better known not for his conquests but for his famous law codes. Interestingly, these law codes probably did not function as legal guidelines for the magistrates of the empire (such as our legal codes today). Instead, they were semireligious texts, demonstrating to Hammurabi's gods (and the people as well) that he indeed ruled with justice.[7] Not surprisingly, Saddam Hussein has also identified himself with Hammurabi, in addition to Sargon and Nebuchadnezzar. Iraqi government propagandistic art has portrayed him standing beside the Stele of Hammurabi (a stele is a stone monument, often with written text on it), which contains the ancient king's famous law codes.[8] The connection is highly ironic, because in the stele Hammurabi boasts of the justice and fairness with which he ruled Babylonia. Although many terms come to mind when one thinks of Saddam's brutal reign of terror in Iraq, justice is not generally one of them.

The "Conqueror of the Jews": Nebuchadnezzar and Neo-Babylonia

Not long after the death of Hammurabi, the fortunes of Babylonia began to decline. For the next several hundred years, an ongoing power struggle ensued in Mesopotamia as numerous nations and migrating groups fought over the rich region. One of the strongest powers to emerge was Assyria, which lay to the north of Babylonia, toward the upstream end of the Tigris-Euphrates region. By 740 B.C., the Assyrians dominated the entire area, and during the next few generations, they extended their control over Syria, Palestine (including the biblical nations of Israel and Judah), and even Egypt. The Assyrians play a major role in the Bible, appearing frequently in 2 Kings and the Book of Isaiah.

However, as the seventh century B.C. progressed, Assyrian power began to wane, and Babylonian power in the southern area of Mesopotamia began to rise again. By this time a fairly large migration of Arameans into Babylonia had taken place, and the main language of the region was Aramaic. This was not the biblical country of Aram, which lay to the west in what is now Syria, but the language was the same. The Chaldeans (see below) and the descendants of these migrating Arameans merged together to become what is known as Neo-Babylonia. This new Babylonia, with its revitalized capital of Babylon, continued to grow in power until it eventually defeated the Assyrians and their Egyptian allies in 612 B.C.

This is the stage of Babylonian history that Saddam dreams of most. Although this empire lasted less than one hundred years (it fell to the Persians in 539 B.C.), Babylon during this time was powerful and spectacular. The Babylonians controlled much of the Middle East, including Mesopotamia, Syria, and Palestine. The most famous Babylonian king of this era was Nebuchadnezzar, and it is this renowned conqueror whom Saddam Hussein likes to identify with most. Nebuchadnezzar was the king who not only built a large empire but also besieged Jerusalem and then destroyed it in 588/87 B.C. He appears in the Bible numerous times, especially in 2 Kings, Jeremiah, and Daniel. He was the one responsible for taking the surviving Jews into exile in Babylonia. Because of his empire-building activities and because he destroyed Jerusalem, Nebuchadnezzar is known from history as "conqueror," "empire-builder," and "destroyer of the Jews," all descriptions that Saddam Hussein desires to embody.

Saddam Hussein wants to be associated with Nebuchadnezzar not only because he was a famous and successful military conqueror but also because he was the one who conquered Jerusalem and carried the Jews into exile. One of Saddam's major aspirations for the last twenty-five years has been to be the leader of the Arab world. His rise to power was closely allied with the pan-Arab movement of the late sixties and early seventies, and he continues to view himself as the leader not just of Iraq but of all Arabs. One of the most powerful unifying elements in the disparate Arab world is their opposition to the state of Israel. Saddam has a certain amount of clever political savvy (he could not have survived in the brutal world of Iraqi politics without it), and he uses the Nebuchadnezzar image to try to unite not only his own divided people but all Arabs behind him. Although Saddam was very popular throughout the Arab world twenty-five years ago, his popularity has waned in recent years. He is still popular in some Arab circles, but many Arabs today simply do not trust him, even though they may support his defiance of the West and his opposition to Israel.[9]

Who Were the Chaldeans?

In numerous verses of the Bible, some English translations speak of Chaldeans, while in the same verses other translations refer to Babylonians. For example, the King James Version frequently reads *Chaldea* or *Chaldean,* while the New International Version reads *Babylonia* or *Babylonian.* The variation can be confusing, but the explanation is fairly simple. Chaldea refers to a small region just to the south of Babylonia. The Chaldeans formed a critical element of the power base that propelled the Neo-Babylonian Empire to world dominance. In fact, the dynasty that produced Nebuchadnezzar and brought Babylonia to the world stage was Chaldean. In essence, therefore, the people who ruled the Neo-Babylonian Empire could be called either Babylonians or Chaldeans. During much of the biblical period, the terms *Babylonia* and *Chaldea* were synonymous and interchangeable. For the sake of clarity, translations such as the NIV used the better-known term *Babylonia,* but both terms refer to the same place and the same people.

Saddam's Other Megalomaniacal Dreams

As mentioned above, Nebuchadnezzar is not the only famous ancient person with whom Saddam identifies. Using the government's media, over which Saddam has complete control, he has portrayed himself as the embodiment of both King Hammurabi of the Old Babylonian Empire and King Sargon of Akkad, as well as other famous Arab personages. In an attempt to bring the Shias (see chapter 8) under his control, he has even claimed descent from the Ali Bin Abi Taleb, the prophet Mohammed's cousin and a central player in the history of the schism within Islam.[10]

26

Strangely, however, when Saddam became president in 1979, he temporarily dispensed with his identification with the Mesopotamian and Arab personages. His media began calling him "knight," "leader," "struggler," and "son of the people." The Iraqi media also compared him to Peter the Great (A.D. 1672–1725), famous czar of Russian history.[11]

When Saddam became embroiled in the devastating war with Iran (Persia), his media again connected him with famous Mesopotamian and Arab persons, at first depicting him as the famous Arab general Sa'ad Ibn Al Waqqas, who defeated the Persians in the battle of Qadisiya in A.D. 636. In fact, Saïd Aburish, an Arab writer, notes that when the Iraq-Iran war began in 1980, this propaganda campaign increased to "over-kill" proportions. In Iraq, Saddam was everywhere depicted as the "living reincarnation" of dozens of Arab and Mesopotamian leaders. Aburish writes:

> Words and images presenting Saddam as one or other of these historical personalities appeared everywhere, naturally in addition to millions of posters depicting him as a tough general carrying a sidearm or a simple Arab in full Bedouin regalia. Moreover, Saddam's pictures, unlike those of other dictators, were unavoidable—they were present on household items, on clocks, and daily on the front page of every newspaper and in the lead story of every television news programme. It was over-kill. Whatever the concerns of the average Iraqi, Saddam appeared in the guise of a historical figure to solve them.[12]

Conclusion

It is undeniable that Saddam Hussein reconstructed a model of ancient Babylon on the original site and that he uses his government-controlled media frequently to identify himself with the famous Babylonian king Nebuchadnezzar. Nebuchadnezzar was not only a military conqueror but also the one who vanquished the Jews, elements of a reputation that Saddam relishes. Yet Saddam has also tried to identify himself with practically every great Mesopotamian and Arab leader (and even the Russian czar Peter the Great) in an attempt to unite the Iraqi people behind him and to create a larger-than-life heroic image of himself. Thus, Saddam's identification with Nebuchadnezzar and his related interest in Babylon are not particularly unique. He has tried to connect himself with practically every significant historical leader from the region. We need to keep this in mind and not overemphasize his interest in Nebuchadnezzar and Babylon to the exclusion of his other megalomaniacal dreams.

THREE

The Biblical Nemesis of Israel

■

Without doubt, the city of Babylon, the country of Babylonia, and the Babylonian people play a large role in the Bible. In fact, the terms *Babylon, Babylonian, Chaldea,* and *Chaldean* appear over three hundred times in the Bible. The vast majority of these terms occur in the Old Testament, and the bulk of the references are found in 2 Kings, Isaiah, and Jeremiah, although references are scattered throughout, including Genesis, as discussed below. This chapter explores the role Babylon played in the Old Testament, primarily in the books of Isaiah and Jeremiah, and also traces the resultant history of Babylon. What actually happened to Babylon after the Old Testament prophets predicted her destruction?

The Tower of Babel

Although most of the references to Babylon occur in 2 Kings, Isaiah, and Jeremiah, a few texts in Genesis refer to or allude to Babylon. Genesis 2:14 names two of the rivers flowing out of the Garden of Eden as the Tigris and the Euphrates. However, this text is complicated by the mention of two other rivers, the Pishon and the Gihon, whose locations are uncertain. Likewise, Genesis 10:10 states that Babylon was one of the first centers of the kingdom of the mighty warrior Nimrod, but the puzzling nature of Nimrod and the difficulties encountered in interpreting Genesis 10 make it difficult to state much about this reference with certainty.[1]

The third and most famous incident in Genesis regarding Babylon is the story of the tower of Babel:

> They said to each other, "Come, let's make bricks and bake them thoroughly." They used brick instead of stone, and tar for mortar. Then they said, "Come, let us build ourselves a city, with a tower that reaches to the heavens, so that we may make a name for ourselves and not be scattered over the face of the whole earth."
>
> 11:3–4

There are echoes of Genesis 9:1–7 in this passage, for in that text God commanded Noah and his family to *scatter* over the earth and to replenish its population. The builders of the tower of Babel, therefore, were doing just the opposite of the divine injunction.

The tower of Babel was located in "a plain of Shinar" (Gen. 10:10; 11:2; 14:1), the broad alluvial plain of the Tigris and Euphrates Rivers south of modern Baghdad.[2] Most likely, the tower of Babel was a ziggurat (an elevated temple tower with stairs), which worshipers climbed to offer sacrifices to their gods. At the top of the ziggurat was a temple shrine known as the gateway to the gods. It was there that humans and the deities supposedly met. In the language of Mesopotamia, Babel (as well as Babylon) meant "gateway to the gods" or "gate of the gods." In Hebrew, however, the word *babel* means "to confuse." Genesis 11:9 thus contains a parody, or wordplay, on the name Babel. It does not really refer to the gate of the gods, as the Mesopotamians intended; rather, it is an allusion to the confusion and scattering that God brought against them. Thus, rather than reaching to the heavens, the tower was abandoned in its construction because God turned the language of the builders into babel, confusion.

From early in Scripture, therefore, Babel and Babylon carry negative connotations. Indeed, later in biblical Israel's history, the city of Babylon will again carry a negative connotation as a sign for human arrogance and rebellion against God.

The Babylonian Destruction of Jerusalem

When God delivered the children of Israel from Egypt during the time of Moses, he made a covenant with them and led them to the Promised Land. In the Book of Deuteronomy, God spelled out the terms by which the Israelites could live in the land and be blessed by God. They were commanded to be faithful to God alone and to worship him alone. If they failed to be faithful to God, the Book of Deuteronomy warned (see especially chapter 28), God would punish them with foreign invasions (among other things), and ultimately they would be evicted from the Promised Land.

Unfortunately, by and large, the Israelites ignored God's warning, and as time went on, they began to worship other gods. The northern ten tribes broke off and formed the country of Israel, while the southern tribes of Judah and Benjamin formed the country of Judah. The northern tribes fell immediately into apostasy and worshiped golden calves. Judah eventually followed suit, worshiping the pagan gods of the Canaanites and their other neighbors. The Old Testament prophets (Isaiah, Jeremiah, Micah, etc.) preached against this serious backsliding of God's people and called the people to repent. But they also warned of imminent judgment on the people if they did not repent. The prophets first warned the northern kingdom of Israel, but Israel ignored them. Therefore, as the prophets predicted, the Assyrians invaded and destroyed the northern kingdom of Israel (722 B.C.). They carried off most of the people and scattered them throughout the Middle East.

The prophets then preached to the southern kingdom of Judah, warning the people of serious consequences if they continued to ignore God and to worship other deities. Failure to repent, the prophets warned, would result in an invasion and terrible destruction by the Babylonians. The prophet Jeremiah was at the center of this message, for he lived through the terrible times of spiritual decline and actually witnessed the horrendous Babylonian invasion. The Book of Jeremiah thus refers to the Babylonians 198 times. In chapters 20 to 39, Jeremiah warned the people of Jerusalem that God would raise up the Babylonians to judge them. When the Babylonians finally arrived and the city came under siege, Jeremiah urged the people of Jerusalem to surrender and thus save themselves, because otherwise they would be destroyed. They could not overcome the ones whom God had raised up to judge them. Jeremiah preached in vain, however, and chapters 40 to 49 describe the fall of Jerusalem to Nebuchadnezzar and his Babylonian army and the resulting devastation. Second Kings 24–25 tells the same grim story. In 587 B.C., Nebuchadnezzar and his army destroyed Jerusalem, burning the city and the temple to the ground. They then carried most of the population into exile in Babylonia.

This terrible event remained etched in the minds of the Old Testament writers, and Babylon became the literary symbol and epitome of Israel's enemies. No other foe wreaked such havoc and destruction on Jerusalem as did the Babylonians.

The Old Testament Prophecies against Babylon

Accordingly, the Old Testament prophets not only preached judgment on Israel and Judah because of their apostasy but also prophesied judgment on the surrounding pagan nations that had exploited Israel and Judah or had directly attacked them. Thus, Jeremiah, for example, prophesied against Egypt (46:1–28), Philistia (47:1–7), Moab (48:1–47), Ammon (49:1–6), Edom (49: 7–22), Damascus (49:23–27), the Arab cities of Kedar and Hazor (49:28–33), Elam (49:34–39), and also Babylon (50:1–51:58).

Because of the devastation the Babylonians brought to Jerusalem, and because Babylon set herself against God, the Lord spoke through the prophet Jeremiah to announce judgment on Babylon:

> Announce and proclaim among the nations,
> lift up a banner and proclaim it;
> keep nothing back, but say,

"Babylon will be captured. . . .
   Her images will be put to shame
   and her idols filled with terror."
A nation from the north will attack her
   and lay waste her land.
No one will live in it;
   both men and animals will flee away.

50:2–3

Take up your positions around Babylon,
   all you who draw the bow.
Shoot at her! Spare no arrows,
   for she has sinned against the LORD.

50:14

So desert creatures and hyenas will live there,
   and there the owl will dwell.
It will never again be inhabited
   or lived in from generation to generation.

50:39

Isaiah also proclaimed a scathing indictment on Babylon and announced a coming judgment on the Babylonians. Isaiah devoted a considerable amount of his book to this theme; the Babylonian judgment fills most of chapters 13, 14, 21, and 47. For example, in Isaiah 13:19–20, the prophet declares:

Babylon, the jewel of kingdoms,
   the glory of the Babylonians' pride,
will be overthrown by God
   like Sodom and Gomorrah.
She will never be inhabited
   or lived in through all generations;

no Arab will pitch his tent there,
no shepherd will rest his flocks there.

Likewise, in Isaiah 21:9, the prophet envisions the declaration of Babylon's destruction:

> Look, here comes a man in a chariot
> with a team of horses.
> And he gives back the answer:
> "Babylon has fallen, has fallen!
> All the images of its gods
> lie shattered on the ground!"

Both Jeremiah and Isaiah, therefore, developed the description of Babylon's destruction into a major theme. Jeremiah spent at least two chapters on this theme (50–51), and Isaiah spent nearly four (13, 14, 21, 47). Obviously, this was an important aspect of the prophetic message.

The Fall and Destruction of Babylon

What actually happened to Babylon? When Jeremiah proclaimed the coming judgment on Babylon, the city was perhaps the most spectacular and most powerful city in the world. Yet when German archaeologists began excavations of Babylon in 1899, the entire site was desolate and unoccupied.[3] What happened to the city between the time of Jeremiah and the era of modern archaeology? A brief overview of Babylon's history since the time of Jeremiah and Nebuchadnezzar is as follows.

Nabonidus, the king who followed Nebuchadnezzar, tried to move the Babylonians away from the worship of their main god, Marduk, and this attempt alienated him from much of the population. Nabonidus even moved to Arabia for ten years, leaving his son Belshazzar in charge. When Cyrus the Persian began to threaten Babylonia, Nabonidus returned to Babylon, but it was too late. One of the most powerful Babylonian princes, Ugbaru, defected to the Persians, allowing Cyrus to defeat the Babylonians in 539 B.C. and to take control of Babylon without meeting any substantial resistance from the city. The inhabitants of Babylon greeted Cyrus more as a liberator than a conqueror. Still, this was the beginning of the end for Babylon.

Later, Babylon revolted against the Persians, but Xerxes recaptured the city for Persia in 482 B.C., sacking it, demolishing its fortifications, burning the great temple of Marduk (Babylonia's most important deity), and carrying away the statue of Marduk as a spoil of war. Those who remained in Babylon were severely taxed, and many homes and estates were confiscated. Yet Herodotus (450 B.C.), the Greek historian, records that Babylon still was not completely destroyed.

When Alexander the Great and his Greek army defeated the Persians in 331 B.C., the young king treated Babylon with kindness and was therefore warmly welcomed by its remaining citizens. In 324 B.C., however, Alexander's dear friend Hephaestian died, and the young king had a funeral pyre erected in his honor in Babylon. Part of the city wall east of the royal palace was demolished to provide rubble for the platform.

After Alexander's premature death in 323 B.C., one of his four generals, Seleucus, seized Babylon in 312

B.C. A fragmentary Babylonian chronicle records that at that time there was "weeping and mourning in the land" and "plundering of the city and the countryside." Seleucus's successor, Antiochus I (281–261 B.C.), issued two decrees that would eventually seal the fate of Babylon. First, he decided to build a new capital (Seleucia-on-the-Tigris) ninety kilometers to the north of Babylon. Second, the civilian population of Babylon was moved to the new capital. These events, along with the physical damage Babylon had suffered when the Seleucids had first conquered southern Mesopotamia, ensured the increasing desolation and isolation of the once-great capital. Except for a brief period of renewal under Antiochus IV (173 B.C.), Babylon for all practical purposes ceased to exist.

At the time of the Parthian takeover of Mesopotamia, Mithradates II (122 B.C.) apparently found Babylon in ruin. Strabo, the historian and geographer, said as much in 24 B.C. By his time, Babylon had for the most part been abandoned, and only its walls remained. In A.D. 116, the Roman emperor Trajan wintered in Babylon, finding nothing except ruins. Babylon's desolation, like that of Nineveh before it, by now was proverbial. A second-century A.D. piece written by Lucian said that Nineveh had vanished without a trace and that soon men would search in vain for Babylon.[4]

Cyrus the Persian, therefore, first humbled Babylon by capturing it without a fight, and since the invasion of Cyrus, there has never been an independent political entity of Babylonia. Over the next three hundred years, the city of Babylon continued to decline and eventually ceased to exist. By the second century B.C., Babylon was no more; only a desolate ruin remained. In fulfillment of biblical prophecy, the city of Babylon went from being the most important and most spectacular city in the world to being a desolate, insignificant pile of rubble.

Conclusion

From the beginning of the biblical story, Babylon carries negative associations and connotations. First associated with the rebellion against God at the tower of Babel, Babylonia later became the main nemesis of Israel when Nebuchadnezzar destroyed Jerusalem and carried the children of Israel into captivity. However, according to God's plan, as prophesied by the Old Testament prophets, Babylon herself fell under God's judgment and was destroyed. Because of the negative role Babylon played in the history of Israel, later biblical writers used Babylon as a symbol of evil, destruction, and opposition to God's plan. This theme will be discussed and developed in chapter 6.

A question remains, however: Even though, as this chapter described, Babylon has already been destroyed, do the prophecies of the Bible reveal that it must be rebuilt and then destroyed again? This issue will be addressed in the next chapter.

FOUR

Must Babylon Be Destroyed Again?

—

Saddam Hussein is rebuilding a model of ancient Babylon on its original site. Is Saddam fulfilling biblical prophecy with this construction? Even though Babylon fell to Cyrus the Persian in 539 B.C., does the Bible in fact predict that it will be rebuilt and then destroyed again in the end-times?

Several popular writers claim that the fall of Babylon described in the previous chapter did not fulfill the prophecies of Isaiah or Jeremiah. Indeed, the leading proponents of this view, Tim LaHaye, Charles Dyer, and Joseph Chambers, assume (but state quite dogmatically) that Babylon must be rebuilt in order to be destroyed according to the specific details of Isaiah's and Jeremiah's prophecies. They connect this assumption to other end-time prophecies and conclude that this reconstructed Babylon must be the center of the Antichrist's world government. Therefore, they maintain that the reconstruction activities of Saddam Hussein signal the beginning of the end-times.

This thesis received its most extensive development in Charles Dyer's 1991 best-seller, *The Rise of Babylon: Sign of the End Times*. When the Gulf War broke out in 1990, Dyer's predictions looked ominous, and his book sold hundreds of thousands of copies. Even though the Gulf War did not inaugurate the end-times, and even though more than a decade has passed, Dyer and others continue to cling to this view. In a more recent book, Dyer writes, "If you take the Bible at face value, you must conclude that Babylon will achieve a place of international importance in spite of Operation Desert Storm. . . . Babylon will again become the capital of an empire in the Middle East."[1]

Tim LaHaye also rejects the view that an earlier destruction of Babylon was the fulfillment of prophecy. He writes that Babylon not only must be rebuilt but also must become the center of the Antichrist's government. He writes, "Obviously, however, the city must be rebuilt and become the financial capital of the world in order to be destroyed." LaHaye then makes the unbelievable claim that the United Nations headquarters will be moved to Babylon and will become the satanic world government of the end-times. If that were not preposterous enough, LaHaye also states that the United Nations will fund the reconstruction by levying a tax on financial transactions, oil, airport landing fees, "and much more."[2]

Likewise, Joseph Chambers, a proponent of this view, writes:

A few brave souls have preached that the prophesied destruction of Babylon is yet future. Most Bible Scholars have chosen the least controversial route of the convenient interpretation. They have taught that the great prediction of her destruction was complete and this city would never have a future. They cited such passages as, "And Babylon, the glory of kingdoms, the beauty of the Chaldees' excellency, shall be as when God overthrew Sodom and Gomorrah. It shall never be inhabited, neither shall it be dwelt in from generation to generation: neither shall the Arabian pitch tent there; neither shall the shepherds make their fold there" (Isa. 13:19–20). It certainly sounds convincing on the surface.[3]

Dyer, one of the "few brave souls" that Chambers mentions, offers two basic arguments against the view that Babylon has already been judged and destroyed (the view of the majority of scholars). First and foremost, as mentioned above, he argues that Babylon was never completely destroyed and uninhabited (Isa. 13:19; Jer. 50:44; 51:30, 43).[4] Second, he maintains that the defeat of Babylon is associated with the Old Testament concept of the day of the Lord, which is equated with the future great tribulation (Isa. 13:1–6) and thus could not have already happened.[5] Are LaHaye, Chambers, and Dyer correct?

The Language of Destruction

First of all, it should be noted that when LaHaye and Dyer argue that Babylon has not yet been destroyed in the manner described by biblical prophecy, their arguments are based on a literalistic and "wooden" reading of the poetic prophetic texts. The prophets are indeed

41

predicting actual future events, but they consistently use figurative language to describe those events. Forcing a rigid, overly literal interpretation on this type of language leads to a meaning that the biblical authors did not intend.

For example, the prophet Amos speaks of the wrath of God when he says, "The lion has roared" (Amos 3:8). Does a literal, cosmic-sized lion need to roar against Israel for this verse to be fulfilled? Obviously not, for clearly the verse depicts God in a figurative fashion. The wrath and anger of God are literally true, but they are portrayed using the colorful imagery of a hungry, roaring lion.

The prophets use figures of speech constantly to convey the literal events they predict. Thus, the fall of Babylon was a real event that they predicted and announced, but their description of that fall is clearly figurative. Taking these judgmental texts literally can lead to a faulty understanding and bad theology. For instance, as part of his prophecy against Babylon, Jeremiah states, "Babylon will be captured; Bel will be put to shame, Marduk filled with terror" (50:2). Bel and Marduk were the pagan gods the Babylonians worshiped. Does this prophecy demand that a real divine being named Bel and a real divine being named Marduk need to be created so they can literally be put to shame and filled with terror? Does the Bible teach polytheism? Clearly not. The prophet speaks of these pagan deities figuratively. When Babylon falls, her "gods" will figuratively be shamed and filled with terror.

Dyer and LaHaye insist that Babylon will be rebuilt because it was not destroyed according to the literal details given in Jeremiah and Isaiah. Do Dyer and

LaHaye mean to say that all the prophecies given by Jeremiah and Isaiah against Babylon will be fulfilled literally in the future?

Let's examine some other prophecies of Jeremiah and Isaiah and consider the plausibility of Dyer and LaHaye's proposal. Consider, for example, the military equipment described in Isaiah and Jeremiah. The attack against Babylon is described repeatedly by the prophets as an attack by archers and swordsmen. "Summon archers against Babylon, all those who draw the bow" (Jer. 50:29). "Sharpen the arrows, take up the shields!" (Jer. 51:11). "Her warriors will be captured, and their bows will be broken" (Jer. 51:56). Will the future battle that destroys the Iraqi city of Babylon be fought with bows and arrows? Dyer and LaHaye's overly literalistic approach, which ignores normal figures of speech, seems to demand that it will.

Likewise, consider Isaiah 21:9: "Look, here comes a man in a chariot with a team of horses. And he gives back the answer: 'Babylon has fallen, has fallen!'" Will the messenger who announces the fall of Babylon travel by chariot? If one insists on a literal reading of the entire prophecy about the fall of Babylon, one ends up with some very unlikely future situations. Does it not seem more reasonable and more in line with proper interpretation to take much of the prophecy as a figurative description of Babylon's fall rather than as a literal one? If the terms *sword, spear, arrow, bow,* and *chariot* are understood literally, then a very bizarre picture emerges of an end-time twenty-first-century A.D. battle fought with sixth-century B.C. implements of war. If taken figuratively, however, as most Old Testament scholars understand the text, these prophecies predict the spectacular fall of Babylon and the Babylonian Empire, but the predictions are not a literal description of the details. Consider a modern example. Suppose that the night before a game, a football fan from the University of Oklahoma says to a rival fan at the University of Nebraska, "Our team is going to stomp your team into the ground! We are going to chew you up and spit you out! We are going to mow down the cornfields of Nebraska, and you will be too embarrassed ever to show your face around here again!" No one today takes this prediction in a literalistic fashion. Clearly, what the rowdy fan from OU is predicting is complete and total victory, not cannibalism. The Old Testament prophets are speaking in much the same manner about Babylon, except, of course, that they have God behind them, and he intends to carry out their prophecy.

God's Reasons for the Judgment and His Timing

Several other compelling reasons exist for believing that the fulfillment of the judgment prophecies on Babylon began with Cyrus and was completed within a few hundred years after Cyrus. The reason God judged Babylon is stated clearly in both Isaiah and Jeremiah. In 587 B.C., the Babylonians devastated Judah and burned Jerusalem to the ground, destroying the temple and exiling the surviving inhabitants. This event is clearly the cause for the punishment of Babylon, as stated numerous times in Jeremiah (50:11–17, 28–29, 33–34; 51:10–11, 24, 35–36, 49, 56). Does it make sense that God would now carry out this punishment on the twenty-first-century Iraqi city of Babylon? The people of Iraq are not Babylonians (see chapter 8). Although ethnically Iraq is diverse, the majority of the population is Arab. Does it make sense to punish Arabs in the twenty-first century for what the Babylonians did to Jerusalem in 587 B.C.? Does it not make more sense to see the punishment as that inflicted by Cyrus on the Babylonians starting in 539 B.C.?

Is God's Prophetic Judgment Ever Conditional?

God certainly brings about all the future events he decrees. However, God himself teaches that some of his judgment announcements have conditional elements— that is, the specific fulfillment of a judgment is conditioned on the response of those under judgment. God states this clearly in Jeremiah 18:7–8:

> If at any time I announce that a nation or kingdom is to be uprooted, torn down and destroyed, and if that nation I warned repents of its evil, then I will relent and not inflict on it the disaster I had planned.

Therefore, the reaction of those under judgment can indeed affect the implementation of the judgment. This truth is illustrated in the familiar story of Jonah and Nineveh, the capital of ancient Assyria. At God's insistence, Jonah proclaimed judgment on Nineveh, saying, "Forty more days and Nineveh will be overturned" (Jonah 3:4). The Ninevites repented of their evil, and God relented and did not destroy them after forty days.

These particular Ninevites apparently repented of their evil and thus were spared God's judgment. However, biblical history shows that the city as a whole did not turn to God, and later generations of Assyrians were again hostile toward God and his people. Ultimately, Assyria and Nineveh were totally destroyed (in 612 B.C. by the Babylonians), and God indicates that this was due to his judgment. In fact, in Jeremiah 50:18, God compares the prophesied judgment on Babylon to that which he brought on Assyria. Thus, God states, "I will punish the king of Babylon and his land as I punished the king of Assyria."

Does the king of Babylon ever repent or acknowledge God? He comes pretty close, and the Book of Daniel records several interesting instances. These texts are discussed in more detail in chapter 6, but some of these verses bear repeating here as well. In Daniel 3, after King Nebuchadnezzar sees four men walking around in the fiery furnace, notice what happens:

> Then Nebuchadnezzar said, "Praise be to the God of Shadrach, Meshach and Abednego, who has sent his angel and rescued his servants! They trusted in him and defied the king's command and were willing to give up their lives rather than serve or worship any god except their own God. Therefore I decree that the people of any nation or language who say anything against the God of Shadrach, Meshach and Abednego be cut into pieces and their houses be turned into piles of rubble, for no other god can save in this way." Then the king promoted Shadrach, Meshach and Abednego in the province of Babylon.
>
> vv. 28–30

Even more significant is Daniel 4, for after God strikes Nebuchadnezzar with insanity, the following occurs:

> At the end of that time, I, Nebuchadnezzar, raised my eyes toward heaven, and my sanity was restored. Then

46

I praised the Most High; I honored and glorified him who lives forever. His dominion is an eternal dominion; his kingdom endures from generation to generation. All the peoples of the earth are regarded as nothing. He does as he pleases with the powers of heaven and the peoples of the earth. No one can hold back his hand or say to him: "What have you done?" At the same time that my sanity was restored, my honor and splendor were returned to me for the glory of my kingdom. My advisers and nobles sought me out, and I was restored to my throne and became even greater than before. Now I, Nebuchadnezzar, praise and exalt and glorify the King of heaven, because everything he does is right and all his ways are just. And those who walk in pride he is able to humble.

vv. 34–37

These statements certainly seem to reflect a humbling of the proud Nebuchadnezzar of Babylon. They seem to indicate that he did change his attitude toward the God of Daniel and become repentant, at least to some degree. As in the case of Nineveh, God was ready to respond with grace. He is apparently always willing to modify judgment based on the repentant attitude of people.

Jeremiah the prophet preached to Jerusalem for years and years, proclaiming that the Babylonians would come in judgment and destroy the city, killing many of the inhabitants. However, when Nebuchadnezzar appears and lays siege to Jerusalem, Jeremiah tells the people that if they surrender to Nebuchadnezzar, thus acknowledging that he is bringing about God's judgment, they will live (Jer. 38:2). The city will still be under judgment and will still be captured, Jeremiah proclaims (38:3), but many of the people will live, implying that the

47

consequences of the judgment will not be as severe. This text in Jeremiah is interesting because the Babylonians later do what Jeremiah encouraged the Jerusalemites to do—surrender to the agent of God's judgment, the conquering invader. The Israelites in Jerusalem refuse and are completely destroyed. The Babylonians, however, in contrast to Jerusalem, surrender to Cyrus without resistance, and thus that generation is not completely destroyed by Cyrus. The judgment still came eventually, and over the next several hundred years, Babylon was completely destroyed, but perhaps their decision to surrender to God's agent of destruction modified the judgment to some extent, as had happened in Nineveh.

Does Cyrus Fulfill the Prophecy against Babylon?

Although the above arguments are convincing in and of themselves, there are additional reasons why the vast majority of scholars in the field of Old Testament studies maintains that the prophesied judgment on Babylon has already taken place. Indeed, one of the most decisive reasons for believing this view is that the Bible states this fact fairly clearly.

Cyrus plays an important role in the prophecies of Isaiah. First of all, Isaiah proclaims that Cyrus will be the one who allows the Jews to return and rebuild the Jerusalem that Nebuchadnezzar destroyed. Thus, in Isaiah 44, the Lord says of Cyrus, "He is my shepherd and will accomplish all that I please; he will say of Jerusalem, 'Let it be rebuilt'" (v. 28). In the next chapter, Isaiah identifies Cyrus as the one God has chosen to conquer nations: "This is what the LORD says to his anointed, to Cyrus, whose right hand I take hold of to subdue nations before him" (45:1). After identifying Cyrus as an agent of God's wrath in Isaiah 44 and 45, the prophet describes the destruction of Babylon in Isaiah 46 and 47. In Isaiah 48, Cyrus is implicitly connected to that destruction of Babylon as the prophet brings together the identity of God's agent (Cyrus) and the prophecy of Babylon's destruction. Isaiah 48:14–15 thus reads, "The LORD's chosen ally will carry out his purpose against Babylon; his arm will be against the Babylonians. I, even I, have spoken; yes, I have called him. I will bring him, and he will succeed in his mission."

It is important to underscore that every significant scholarly commentator on Isaiah, conservative and nonconservative alike, past and present, believes that Isaiah 48:14–15 refers to Cyrus.[6] Cyrus fulfilled Isaiah's prophecies about the destruction of Babylon. Babylon was conquered by Cyrus and shortly thereafter fell into ruin and disuse. There is no reason to assume that Babylon must be rebuilt in order for these prophecies to be fulfilled. These verses are a serious rebuttal of the view of Dyer, Chambers, and LaHaye, who have popularized the view that the prophesies of Isaiah concerning Babylon were not fulfilled by Cyrus and thus must take place in the future.

The Medes Are Also Involved

Another important group of prophetic verses that refer to the destruction of Babylon implicates the Medes as part of the conquering army. Jeremiah 51:11 states, "Sharpen the arrows, take up the shields! The LORD has stirred up the kings of the Medes, because his purpose is to destroy Babylon!"

Likewise, Jeremiah 51:28–29 repeats this identification:

> Prepare the nations for battle against her—
>   the kings of the Medes,
> their governors and all their officials,
>   and all the countries they rule.
> The land trembles and writhes,
>   for the LORD's purposes against Babylon stand—
> to lay waste the land of Babylon
>   so that no one will live there.

Isaiah's prophecy against Babylon in Isaiah 13 makes the same connection, identifying the Medes as the ones who will strike judgment on Babylon: "See, I will stir up against them [i.e., the Babylonians] the Medes" (v. 17). Isaiah also identifies the Medes as the punishing agent of the judgment on Babylon in Isaiah 21:2.

The Medes inhabited the area that is now southern Iran. When the Babylonians rose up to challenge the Assyrians, the Medes, who were in control of most of Persia, allied themselves with the Babylonians in their successful attack in 612 B.C. During the years that followed, the Persians, although once under the Medes' control, grew strong and overthrew the Median rulers. However, as Edwin Yamauchi describes in his important book *Persia and the Bible,* Cyrus the Persian defeated the Medes and absorbed them into his kingdom, blurring the terminological distinction between the Medes and the Persians. In the same manner that the terms *Babylonian* and *Chaldean* became synonymous, the terms *Mede* and *Persian* became synonymous, or at least very similar in meaning. For example, in several places in the Book of Daniel (6:8, 12, 15; 8:20) and in the Book of Esther (1:3, 14), the phrase "Medes and Persians" (or "Media and Persia") is used, indicating the close association of the two. Yamauchi explains that in biblical usage the terms are synonymous and interchangeable. Thus, he states that the reference to the Medes by Isaiah and Jeremiah as the destroyers of Babylon is a reference to the Persians as well.[7] This, of course, also coincides with the references to Cyrus discussed above.

The prophets Isaiah and Jeremiah are very clear in their prophecy concerning Babylon. The city of Babylon would indeed be conquered and humbled and ultimately destroyed. The ones responsible would be Cyrus and also the Medes (his Medo-Persian empire). Thus, the biblical evidence is rather overwhelming that this prophecy was fulfilled by Cyrus in the sixth century B.C. It does not await a future fulfillment by the armies of modern countries.

The Day of the Lord

The same evaluation can be made of the other arguments that the Bible predicts a future rise and final destruction of Babylon. Thus, Dyer's second point—that the fall of Babylon is associated with the day of the Lord and will not happen until the future great tribulation—proves to be misguided. In the Old Testament, the day of the Lord refers to those times when God intervenes in history to judge Israel and/or the nations and to bring about his purpose. It includes future judgment and end-time events, but it also includes earlier judgments and actions of God (i.e., the destruction of Israel in 722 B.C. and Judah in 587 B.C.). This understanding is held by most serious Old Testament scholars.[8]

51

Thus, associating the destruction of Babylon with the day of the Lord is in keeping with Old Testament usage, and such destruction can be equated with God's intervening judgment on the earth. It does not explicitly refer to the great tribulation (contra LaHaye and Dyer). The destruction of Israel (722 B.C.) and the destruction of Jerusalem (587 B.C.) were likewise prophesied as part of the day of the Lord. Therefore, to include the destruction of Babylon (begun in 539 B.C.) as part of the day of the Lord reflects a normal usage of that term. It does not require future association with end-time judgment.

LaHaye and the Rabbis

In their recent book *Are We Living in the End Times?* Tim LaHaye and Jerry Jenkins make a puzzling connection between ancient rabbinic interpretation and the rebuilding of Babylon. They write, "An ancient rabbinic rule of interpretation says that when the Bible mentions an event twice, it means the event will happen twice." Then they note that Isaiah 21:9 says, "Babylon has fallen, has fallen!" Likewise, they observe that in the Book of Revelation John writes, "Fallen! Fallen is Babylon the Great" (14:8). LaHaye and Jenkins then conclude, "Since the word 'fallen' is used twice in each of these passages, the rabbinic rule demands that the city fall twice."[9]

Needless to say, this claim by LaHaye and Jenkins is probably one of the most outlandish, misleading, and inaccurate statements in current literature relating to prophecy. First of all, LaHaye and Jenkins do not cite the rabbinic source or even say where they read this.

Second, rabbinic interpretation was a *Jewish* method of reading the Hebrew Bible (i.e., the Old Testament) that largely developed after the time of Christ. The earliest rabbinic literature dates to the third century A.D., centuries after the time of Christ. What relevance do Jewish rules of interpretation from the third century A.D. have for Christians today? Rabbinic rules of interpretation were often used by the rabbis to argue against the Christian claim that Jesus was the Messiah. The Jewish rabbinic method of interpreting Scripture often differs radically from the way Christians interpret Scripture. For LaHaye and Jenkins to suggest that a Jewish rabbinic rule of interpretation should guide Christians today in their reading of the Bible flies in the face of normal Christian interpretation methods.

The icing on this cake of absurdity is their application of the Jewish rabbinic rule of interpretation to the Book of Revelation, a Christian book that is not part of the Jewish canon. Applying Jewish rabbinic rules of interpretation to both the New Testament and the Old Testament is a particularly poor interpretive method for Christians to use.

Finally, it should be noted that the repetition of terms or phrases is fairly common in the Bible, especially in the Old Testament. The repetition of a term or phrase signifies a stress or emphasis on that term or phrase. It has nothing to do with something being completed twice. This understanding is fairly standard among Old Testament scholars and those who teach Hebrew. Thus, in Isaiah 21:9, the repeated phrase "Babylon has fallen, has fallen!" simply reflects a strong emphasis on that fact.

Conclusion

Because the Babylonians invaded Judah and ruthlessly destroyed Jerusalem and the temple, God announced judgment on them. In particular, the prophets Isaiah and Jeremiah predicted the downfall of Babylon. In fulfillment of these prophecies, Babylonia was dismantled, and the city of Babylon fell to Cyrus the Persian. Over the next few hundred years, the fortunes of Babylon continued to deteriorate until the city effectively disappeared, remaining only as a forsaken ruin, a mere reminder of the reversal of fortunes that overtook the city due to its opposition to God.

Thus, the fall of Babylon that began in 539 B.C. did indeed fulfill the prophecies of judgment made against that city by the Old Testament prophets. These prophecies do not demand that Babylon be rebuilt so that it can be destroyed again. The construction program of Saddam Hussein to build a model of ancient Babylon on the original site is not a prerequisite for fulfillment of Isaiah's or Jeremiah's prophecies. Those prophecies have already been fulfilled.

Does Saddam's new Babylon have anything to say to us about biblical prophecy? Yes. The very fact that Babylon has been in ruins for centuries bears testimony to the judgment of God on that ancient city for its sin and rebellion against him. Saddam's boastful identification with Nebuchadnezzar and his attempt to reconstruct Babylon are filled with irony, for in reality he is only reminding us how brief the existence of the Babylonian Empire was and how complete was God's judgment on it. Much of ancient Babylon still lies in ruins, bearing testimony to the consequences of opposing God.

The reconstruction of Babylon's ancient architecture, whether on site in Babylon or in the museum in Berlin (the famous Ishtar Gate of Babylon was reconstructed in Berlin many years ago) does not signal the rise of ancient Babylon. It merely reminds us that the power of Babylon was brief and has been humbly relegated to the pages of history, to the halls of quiet museums, and to a shoddy tourist attraction in Iraq.

FIVE

The Coming Muslim Invasion of Israel

All Americans have been aware for some time of the tensions between Muslims and Jews in the Middle East. Those who are old enough have vivid memories of the Arab-Israeli wars in 1967 and 1973 and remember the Arab terrorist activities of the 1970s—hijackings, bombings, and the tragic murder of Israeli Olympian athletes. As the Cold War ended, however, we began to hope for peace in the Middle East. The leaders of Israel and Egypt, her most powerful enemy, signed a peace treaty and shook hands. The problem of the Palestinians remained unsettled—a large problem to be sure—but at least the large modern army of Egypt had withdrawn from the powder keg. Terrorism continued, and through the news media we became familiar with groups such as

Hamas, Hezballah, and Abu Nidal, but in general, many Americans felt the problem was a distant one.

The September 11 attack on the World Trade Center changed things drastically for most Americans. It brought the Middle East conflict into our front yard. The terrorists were no longer operating in Netanya; they were in New York. We learned that an Islamic extremist group known as Al Qaeda, led by Osama bin Laden, was intent on waging a terrorist war on Israel and the United States. As American troops landed in Afghanistan, the news media scrambled to educate Americans about radical Islam and its hatred of us because of our support of Israel.

It is not surprising, therefore, that Christian Americans are very interested in the possible role Muslims—particularly those associated with the recent surge of radical Islamic fundamentalism—will play in the end-times. Numerous popular writers, Tim LaHaye and Hal Lindsey, for example, have proclaimed that the prophecies of Ezekiel 38–39 refer to an invasion of Israel by a Muslim coalition. Furthermore, they see this invasion as imminent and as part of the rapidly unfolding sequence of end-time events. Several of these writers argue that Russia will lead or at least assist this Muslim coalition of countries against Israel. Because the United States is at the present time deeply involved in the morass of Middle Eastern politics and tragedy, it is imperative that we know if these writers are correct or not. Does the Bible teach that various Middle Eastern Muslim countries will unite within the next few years and invade Israel? If so, where do Babylon and Iraq fit in? Also, do all biblical scholars believe this will happen?

The Prophecy of the End-Time Invasion

The prophet Ezekiel, preaching sometime between 598 and 587 B.C., paints a picture of a hostile attack against a peaceful, regathered Israel. In chapter 38, he states:

> The word of the LORD came to me: "Son of man, set your face against Gog, of the land of Magog, the chief prince of Meshech and Tubal; prophesy against him and say: 'This is what the Sovereign LORD says: I am against you, O Gog, chief prince of Meshech and Tubal. I will turn you around, put hooks in your jaws and bring you out with your whole army—your horses, your horsemen fully armed, and a great horde with large and small shields, all of them brandishing their swords. Persia, Cush and Put will be with them, all with shields and helmets, also Gomer with all its troops, and Beth Togarmah from the far north with all its troops—the many nations with you.
>
> "'Get ready; be prepared, you and all the hordes gathered about you, and take command of them. After many days you will be called to arms. In future years you will invade a land that has recovered from war, whose people were gathered from many nations to the mountains of Israel, which had long been desolate. They had been brought out from the nations, and now all of them live in safety. You and all your troops and the many nations with you will go up, advancing like a storm; you will be like a cloud covering the land.
>
> "'This is what the Sovereign LORD says: On that day thoughts will come into your mind and you will devise an evil scheme. You will say, "I will invade a land of unwalled villages; I will attack a peaceful and unsuspecting people—all of them living without walls and without

gates and bars. I will plunder and loot and turn my hand against the resettled ruins and the people gathered from the nations, rich in livestock and goods, living at the center of the land."'"

vv. 1–12

Throughout the history of the Christian church, writers have tried to interpret Ezekiel 38–39 in light of the events of their own times. Iain Duguid chronicles this attempt throughout history:

> The church father Ambrose, writing in the late fourth century, confidently identified Gog as the Goths. In the seventh century, Gog and Magog were the Arab armies that threatened the Holy Land. By the thirteenth century, Gog had become a cipher for the Mongol hordes from the East. William Greenhill, writing in the seventeenth century, records the opinion of some contemporaries who identified Gog as the Roman emperor, the Pope, or the Turks. In the nineteenth century, against the background of the tensions in Asia Minor that culminated in the Crimean War, Wilhelm Gesenius identified Rosh as Russia. This view was subsequently popularized by the *Scoffield Reference Bible*, along with the idea taken from other sources that "Meshech" and "Tubal" are the Russian cities of Moscow and Tobolsk. During the First World War, Arno Gaebelein argued that Gomer was Germany.[1]

Obviously, throughout history, Christian interpreters have tried to identify the Gog of Ezekiel 38–39 with a geopolitical reality of their day. In hindsight, some of their claims appear to be foolish. Can we learn anything from history? Is there a lesson to be learned that perhaps cautions us against dogmatically identifying people and places in the Bible with current events and people of *our* day? What will the world situation be like in forty years? Will we have enough integrity to admit our mistake if the entire geopolitical situation changes and thus disproves our interpretation?

The Russian-Led Muslim Coalition Theory

Perhaps the most popular writer of biblical prophecy today is Tim LaHaye. In his 1999 book on prophecy, *Are We Living in the End Times?* he and coauthor Jerry Jenkins give their interpretation of Ezekiel 38–39. It is important to note that while the NIV translates Ezekiel 38:2 as, "Gog, of the land of Magog, the chief prince of Meshech and Tubal," the New American Standard version reads, "Gog of the land of Magog, the prince of Rosh, Meshech, and Tubal." The Hebrew word *rosh* means "head, chief." Thus, the NIV identifies Gog as the *chief* prince of Meshech and Tubal, whereas the translators of the NASB understood the word as a proper noun referring to a place called Rosh. Reading the Hebrew word *rosh* as a place (NASB) rather than as the adjective "chief" (NIV), LaHaye and Jenkins believe without a doubt that this passage refers to Russia. The other countries Ezekiel mentions, they argue, are the Arab allies of Russia. With startling and sometimes puzzling proclamations, LaHaye and Jenkins present their case for the Russia-led Muslim coalition theory. Surprisingly (and incorrectly) they also claim widespread scholarly support for the theory. They write:

Few if any prophecy scholars question that the potential fulfillment of this text comes in the end times and that Russia and her allies will go down to the little nation of Israel "to take a spoil."[2]

Etymologically, the Gog and Magog of Ezekiel 38 and 39 can only mean modern-day Russia. . . . What is even more remarkable is that Gog's allies—Persia, Libya, Gomer [thought to be Turkey], Ethiopia, and Togarmah—are all Arab Muslim countries today and they "just happen" to be Russia's faithful allies. Their binding, overriding, passionate, and common hatred is Israel. Indeed, 55 million of Russia's own 250 million people are Arabs, most of whom hate Israel. For centuries prophetic scholars have been convinced that Russia and those who control her will lead the march of the Arab world down to the mountains of Israel.[3]

If Russia is to attack Israel, she had better do it soon! And indications are that Russia is getting ready to do just that. According to many reports coming out of that region of the world, Russia and her Muslim allies are doing everything they can to foment war in Israel. That millions of lives are in jeopardy is inconsequential to them; they want to stamp out Israel at any cost.[4]

There are and always will be differing interpretations of the prophetic texts about the end-times. But LaHaye and Jenkins clearly misunderstand and misrepresent numerous well-known, current-day situations, and their dogmatic statements about current geopolitical reality are wrong. Let's analyze a few of the statements made above and see if this judgment is merited.

Consider the following statements: "Few if any prophecy scholars question that the potential fulfillment of this text comes in the end times and that Russia and her allies will go down to the little nation of Israel 'to take a spoil,'" and "Etymologically, the Gog and Magog of Ezekiel 38 and 39 can only mean modern-day Russia." We will discuss this in more detail below, but let us say here that the vast majority of Old Testament scholars, conservative and nonconservative alike, do not think there is any reference to Russia in Ezekiel's prophecy.[5]

Some of LaHaye's and Jenkins's other statements are even more obviously incorrect. Consider the following: "What is even more remarkable is that Gog's allies—Persia, Libya, Gomer [thought to be Turkey], Ethiopia, and Togarmah—are all Arab Muslim countries today and they 'just happen' to be Russia's faithful allies. Their binding, overriding, passionate, and common hatred is Israel. Indeed, 55 million of Russia's own 250 million people are Arabs, most of whom hate Israel." First of all, the claim that Turkey is a faithful ally of Russia is probably news both to the Turks and to the Russians. On the contrary, Turkey has been a faithful member of NATO and an ally of the United States for quite some time. The Turks sent troops to fight with Americans against communism during the Korean War. They allowed an American-led coalition to use their airfields during the Gulf War, and they again allowed us to use their airfields during the recent operations in Afghanistan. Turkey is Russia's ally? They want to stamp out Israel at any cost? These are preposterous statements.

LaHaye and Jenkins also exhibit a surprising ignorance about Ethiopia. They claim that Ethiopia is an *Arab Muslim* country. One of us (Hays) lived in Ethiopia and worked there as a missionary for five years. The Ethiopians are not Arabs. Ethiopia does have a significant Muslim community, perhaps as high as 30 percent of the population, but those Muslim Ethiopians are not Arabs. And it should be pointed out that the largest religious group in Ethiopia is Christian: the Ethiopian Orthodox Church. Furthermore, the country contains over one million evangelical believers and has a small but well-known Jewish population (the Falashas), many of whom immigrated to Israel in recent years. Imagine how Ethiopian Christians feel when they read these statements by LaHaye and Jenkins. Two famous American Christian writers are proclaiming to America that the Ethiopians are Muslim Arabs and that they have allied themselves with the Muslim world and with the Russians to attack Israel! Ethiopia was under communist rule and was allied with Russia for a brief period in the 1980s. However, they fought a bitter and costly civil war to remove their communist leaders. Christian writers need to be cautious about implicating or accusing faithful Christians in other countries of being part of end-time evil conspiracies.

Jenkins and LaHaye also incorrectly label other people as Arabs. They refer to Turkey and Iran (Persia) as Arab Muslim countries. This is simply incorrect. Equating the terms *Arab* and *Muslim* reflects an uninformed view of the Middle East. Most of the people in Turkey and Iran are Muslims, but they are not Arabs. The Iranians (Persians), in fact, have a long history of hostility toward Arabs, most recently seen in the disastrous Iraq-Iran war of the 1980s. And while the former Soviet Union may have contained fifty-five million Muslims, those people were not Arabs either. Most of those Muslims lived in the southern republics (Kazakhstan, Uzbekistan, etc.) that broke away from

Russia when the Soviet Union unraveled. Currently, only roughly fifteen million Muslims reside in Russia, and they are not Arabs. Furthermore, many of the Muslims who remain in Russia are in Chechnya and are currently in a bitter life and death struggle to gain independence from Russia. They are certainly not allying themselves militarily with Russia. So LaHaye's and Jenkins's statement that Russia today has fifty-five million Muslim Arabs is inaccurate.

Finally, the suggestion that Russia is currently planning an invasion of Israel is outlandish. It makes no geopolitical sense. First of all, the Russian army is but a faint shadow of what the Red Army of the Soviet Union was. Since the end of the Cold War and the breakup of the Soviet Union, Russia has cut its military budget drastically, reducing its number of planes, ships, tanks, and soldiers. Russia no longer has a fleet that can challenge the United States and her allies in the Mediterranean Sea. As long as the United States controls the Mediterranean Sea, Russia cannot possibly send an amphibious force against Israel. On land, to invade Israel, Russia would have to pass through Turkey, which is a NATO ally. Such a move would bring retaliation from NATO. And if a Russian force did manage to get through Turkey, it would be hopelessly outgunned by an American-Israeli alliance.

Economically, such a move would be a disaster for Russia. Russia has tremendous economic problems and continues to look to the West for financial help and investment. An invasion of Israel would consume Russia's limited financial resources and certainly destroy any hope it has of rebuilding its economy.

Another puzzling problem is that of motive. Why would Russia want to jeopardize her economy and tangle with the United States and Israel militarily? Some writers suggest that the Russians need Iranian oil, but that is simply not true. Russia is one of the major oil producers in the world.[6] At the close of 2002, only Saudi Arabia produced more oil than Russia. The Russians are oil exporters, not oil importers. What they need are calm, stable markets and continued development of their oil fields. To suggest, as LaHaye and Jenkins do, that even now the Russians are plotting to invade Israel is ludicrous.

Furthermore, this information, if true, would be front-page news. Is it not strange that the United States intelligence community has said nothing about this? Is it not unusual that the extensive investigative resources of the American (indeed, worldwide) media have not uncovered this plot? Yet LaHaye and Jenkins cite their distorted geopolitical view as *proof* that we are entering the end-times.

This accusation against Russia borders on being irresponsible. If you accuse your neighbor of plotting to rob a bank or commit a murder, you should be able to provide substantial evidence of the plot. LaHaye and Jenkins have accused Russia of a serious crime—plotting to invade Israel. Where is the evidence to substantiate this serious accusation? Needless to say, whether or not one agrees with their understanding of biblical prophecy, it is quite clear that they have seriously misrepresented the geopolitical situation of the day. Because much of their biblical argument rests on their faulty understanding of today's geopolitical situation, the rest of their claims and predictions are questionable as well.

Will Russia Invade Israel at the End of Time?

Who is the foe from the north, and when will it attack Israel? Ezekiel identifies Israel's enemy as "Gog, of the land of Magog, the chief prince of Meshech and Tubal" (Ezek. 38:2). As mentioned above, according to LaHaye and Jenkins and following the popular lead of Hal Lindsey, Gog and Magog denote the Russians, Rosh (chief prince) is Russia, Meshech is Moscow, and Tubal is Tobolsk.[7] Based on this identification, they go on to argue that halfway through the seven-year tribulation period, after Israel has signed a peace pact with the Antichrist (the head of the ten-nation European Common Market), thus accounting for Israel's state of peace in the land, Russia will invade Israel from the north in its last bid for world conquest. However, God will intervene on behalf of his people, the Jews, and will destroy the Russian army. So great will be Russia's destruction that the clean-up operation in the aftermath of the invasion will take seven months. In fact, the fuel from Russia's weapons will burn for seven years!

Some Christians have wondered how the weapons of modern warfare can burn for seven years. LaHaye and Jenkins have the answer, writing, "The Russians have been using Lignostone in the manufacture of many of their weapons of war. Lignostone . . . is stronger than steel . . . and burns better than coal."[8] For documentation they cite a book LaHaye wrote in 1972, hardly proof of what is happening in Russia today, particularly regarding Russian military hardware. Furthermore, Lignostone is a Dutch trademark name for laminated wood (birch) products used primarily in the housing industry and similar to dozens of laminated wood products available in the United States today. Laminated wood products may be useful in constructing barracks, but they are hardly appropriate for weapons.

Let's continue our discussion of Ezekiel 38–39. Although we have already raised several objections to identifying *rosh* as Russia, there are three additional arguments against this view. These arguments relate to grammatical, geographical, and etymological (the development of words) issues.

First, on grammatical grounds, taking the Hebrew term *rosh* as a proper name is debatable. To be sure, some translations follow that approach (the Jerusalem Bible, the New English Bible, and the New American Standard Bible). However, the term can also be rendered as a generic noun—"chief" or "head" prince—as shown in the King James Version, the New Revised Standard Version, the New American Bible, the New International Version, and the New Living Bible. The resulting translation is as follows: "Son of Man, set your face against Gog, the land of Magog, the *chief* prince of Meshech and Tubal." According to this reading, *rosh* is the head of Meshech and Tubal, not another place.

Second, from a geographical perspective, one of the primary reasons writers such as LaHaye and Lindsey equate Russia with the invading foe is because Russia lies directly north of Israel. But as archaeologist Barry Beitzel observes, enemies of ancient Israel, which lay at the bottom of the fertile crescent, attacked from the north regardless of where they resided. For example, Beitzel observes that the Bible describes the following ancient enemies of Israel as being from the north, even though they were located in the east: Assyrians (Zeph.

2:13), Babylonians (Jer. 1:13–15; 6:22; Zech. 2:6–7), Persians (Isa. 41:25; Jer. 50:3).[9]

Third, further damage to the theory that the enemy from the north is Russia comes from the etymological evidence. Historian Edwin Yamauchi notes that even if one transliterates the Hebrew *rosh* as a proper name (as the Septuagint, the Greek translation of the Old Testament does), it can have nothing to do with modern Russia. Yamauchi writes, "This would be a gross anachronism, for the modern name is based upon the name *Rus*, which was brought into the region of Kiev, north of the Black Sea, by the Vikings only in the Middle Ages."[10] Other top evangelical scholars on Ezekiel agree. Daniel Block writes, "The popular identification of Rosh with Russia is impossibly anachronistic and based on a faulty etymology, the assonantal similarities between Russia and Rosh being purely accidental."[11] Iain Duguid concurs, noting that such identification contains several factual flaws and pointing out that Russia is "etymologically unrelated to the Hebrew term."[12]

Yamauchi goes on to analyze the nomenclature "Gog and Magog" and reaches the commonly held scholarly opinion that the antecedents of these historical names cannot be positively identified.[13] However, the identifications of Meshech and Tubal are not in doubt. Few scholars today equate them with Moscow and Tobolsk. Rather, combined ancient testimony attests to the fact that Meshech and Tubal were located in central and eastern Anatolia (Asia Minor), respectively.[14]

The foregoing arguments render the "Russian" hypothesis untenable. The biblical term *rosh* has nothing to do with Russia.

Russians, Muslims, and Changing Horses in Mid-Stream

LaHaye and Lindsey's hypothesis that Russia will invade Israel in the latter days, thus fulfilling Ezekiel 38–39, may have made sense geopolitically when the Soviet Union was a major superpower, but how can this be the case now that the once-mighty empire has collapsed?[15] Lindsey, an author who has written a great deal on the subject, has changed his last-days scenario in light of the Soviet Union's fall. And Lindsey is certainly not alone in changing his analysis of the Soviet Union's role in biblical prophecy. Paul Boyer states that many prognosticators amend their interpretations as political circumstances change and as their predictions are proven untrue or highly unlikely to be fulfilled. He portrays the popular prophecy writers as rather syncretistic in that they include current global events in their prophetic schemes, oftentimes ignoring the fact that new developments contradict their former interpretations. Boyer finds a clear demonstration of this in shifting views on the role of the former Soviet Union and the world of Islam in popular prophetic literature.[16]

Lindsey states in his book *Planet Earth—2000 A.D.* that although the ailing Russia may no longer be a superpower, it will become a dominant force in world affairs because of its nuclear arsenal and will form an alliance with Iran, the leader of the newest major threat to Israel—Islam. This union will be made for two primary reasons: (1) Because Russia needs money to survive and revive its empire, it will sell nuclear arms to Iran; and (2) the strong Islamic presence in the former Soviet republics will force Moscow to enter into a peace pact with Tehran. Together, at Iran's insistence, these two nations will attack Israel, thus fulfilling Ezekiel 38:2–6. In fact, Persia (Iran) will be the "hook in the jaw of Magog" that will draw Magog (Russia) into the ultimate war with Israel known as Armageddon (Ezek. 38:4). The theory is that because of the alliance, Iran, the dominant partner, will force Russia to join in an attack on Israel.[17]

LaHaye and Jenkins still argue for the Russian invasion theory that was popular in the 1970s and 1980s, when the Soviet Union was still a menace to the world. The major modification to their view, because of the collapse of the Soviet Union, is that Russia must attack Israel *soon*, before her nuclear arsenal becomes obsolete and thus worthless. The collapse of the Soviet Union, therefore, does not discredit their view; it merely serves to show how quickly the end is coming. They write, "Either she strikes against Israel in the very near future or she falls into the economic trash bin of history, in which case she would no longer have the capability and the allies to do what the prophet Ezekiel predicted."[18]

Twenty-five years ago Lindsey published *The Late Great Planet Earth,* which has sold millions of copies. In that book he describes in detail the two-flank assault the mighty Soviet forces will make on Israel—a land invasion from the north and an amphibious assault from the Mediterranean Sea. (He saw the buildup of Russian ships in the Mediterranean as a possible sign of the imminence of Armageddon.) The Russians will double-cross their allies in the Islamic Arab confederacy, Lindsey theorized, but the Red Army will be destroyed by nuclear weapons deployed by the Antichrist, who will lead the revived Roman Empire. This was all well and good for 1970, when the book was published, but drastic changes on the global political scene have forced Lindsey and others to change the interpretations in which they had confidence.

How does Lindsey deal with the collapse of a major player in his predictions regarding the last days? He simply changes the story and the roles of the players. For instance, in 1970, Lindsey portrayed Iran as the pawn of the powerful Soviets, who force the "Persians" to ally with them to gain easy military access to the Middle East. In Lindsey's latest interpretations, however, the roles are reversed. The Russians will crawl to Iran to make an alliance in search of financial help and fearing the Islamic presence in Russia. The Russians then are dragged into a war with Israel because of Iran's power. Yet since the Cold War Soviet Union has fallen, it now seems ridiculous to think that Russia can pull off an invasion of the Middle East, much less on two fronts.[19]

Russia and Iran *could* enter into an alliance with each other. But an alliance could be formed—and broken—between any number of nations in these turbulent and unpredictable times. The point is that those who predicted that the Soviet Union would be the great enemy to the north have difficulty acknowledging that the empire is no more. Instead, they amend their interpretations to fit the current scene. Lindsey offers a concluding remark: "Yes, the Evil Empire may be gone, but Russia's role in the end-times scenario remains the same. The mainstream media may not be tracking developments in Russia with much scrutiny and depth or giving them the attention they deserve, but, behind the scenes, there are momentous and profound events taking place in

Moscow. The great bear may not look as dangerous as it once did, but looks can be deceiving."[20] Clearly, Lindsey is rationalizing the error of predicting that a great Soviet military machine will invade Israel on two fronts and will then be powerful enough to break its alliance with an Arab confederacy. He avoids dealing with the reality of the false prediction by saying that the Soviet collapse was inevitable.[21] In what way will future events once again change the theories of prognosticators?

Israel: A Country at Peace without Defenses?

According to the prophecy in Ezekiel 38, when the future attack occurs, Israel will be completely unsuspecting. Ezekiel says that Israel at the time will be a "land that has recovered from war" and that "all of them live in safety" (38:8). He then describes Israel as "a land of unwalled villages . . . a peaceful and unsuspecting people" (38:11). Obviously, this idyllic scene hardly describes Israel today Israel is one of the most heavily defended countries in the world. After the terrors of the Holocaust, the Israelis have vowed that never again will they be caught defenseless. LaHaye and others argue that this peaceful situation described in Ezekiel will be a result of a peace treaty that the new world leader ruling from Babylon will sign with Israel. Ezekiel, however, says nothing about such a treaty.

LaHaye and Jenkins thus predict the following upcoming events: (1) Babylon will be rebuilt and made the capital of a world government (the UN); (2) the leader of this world government will promise peace to Israel, and Israel will believe him, sign a peace treaty, and then disarm; apparently somehow the Palestinian problem is resolved as well; and (3) the Russian-led Muslim coalition will attack the unsuspecting Israel. Note that, as mentioned above, LaHaye and Jenkins have also argued that Russia and her Muslim allies are already planning this invasion, which will happen in our lifetime. If this Russian-led Muslim invasion is obvious to LaHaye and Jenkins, how is Israel to fall for the illusionary peace treaty? Certainly, in the end-times, *anything* can happen, but LaHaye's consistent argument has been that he knows the end-times are upon us precisely because current events have lined up with his interpretation of prophecy. At the present time, however, and for the foreseeable future, it is unlikely that the state of Israel will sign a treaty with the city of Babylon and then disarm based on trust. Also, how likely is Israel to do this precisely at the time that Russia is organizing her so-called Muslim allies to attack her?

Where Are Babylon and Iraq in the Muslim Invasion?

One of the strange things about the end-time Muslim invasion theory is that Babylon does not seem to be directly involved. Ezekiel does not mention Babylon in Ezekiel 38–39, and thus those who advocate the end-time Muslim invasion do not mention the participation of Babylon. Thus, it appears that even though the Iraqi government has threatened Israel for over forty years, often taking the lead among the Arabs in Israel-bashing, when the big Muslim invasion of Israel occurs, the Iraqis will sit it out. The Turks, however, who are currently allies of the United States and members of NATO, will apparently participate in the attack, as will countries such as Uzbekistan, which currently does not appear to have much interest in the Arab-Israeli conflict.

The end-time doomsday writers try to build their arguments by pointing to world events that parallel their interpretations of the biblical description of the end. But it is also important to identify and analyze those aspects in the world today that *differ* significantly from one's interpretation of the biblical picture. The similarities and differences must then be balanced and weighed against other evangelical interpretations of that same biblical picture.

Conclusion

First of all, because of the wide range of views regarding Ezekiel 38–39 held by scholars, people should be cautious about elevating a particular understanding to the level of dogmatic certainty. It is possible that the battle described in Ezekiel 38–39 has already occurred symbolically. However, it is more probable that Ezekiel 38–39 does describe an end-time attack against God's people. However, the nations mentioned (as well as the weapons, etc.) are probably symbolic representations of these enemies and not specific nations that will attack. This is the view suggested by Daniel Block, who writes in his commentary on Ezekiel, "This combination of mystery and brutality made Gog and his confederates perfect symbols of the archetypal enemy rising against God and his people."[22] Iain Duguid in his commentary on Ezekiel advocates a similar view:

> However, even if correct identifications were to be made on the basis of sound linguistic and archaeological data,

attempts to isolate particular nations as "Israel's last enemies" fly in the face of what the text is saying. The point of Ezekiel 38–39 is not that at some distant point in future history these particular nations will oppose Israel. . . . Rather, these seven nations from the ends of the earth, from all four points of the compass, represent symbolically a supreme attempt by the united forces of evil to crush the peace of God's people. This, not coincidentally, is the interpretation given to "Gog and Magog" in Revelation 20:8: They represent "the nations in the four corners of the earth" whom Satan gathers for the final battle against God's people.[23]

Certainly, God will bring into being the plan his prophets proclaimed. However, people should not center their biblical interpretations on themselves and their own particular time in history. And if they are going to point to similarities between an overly literalistic reading of the Bible and current events as proof that the end-times are upon us, they should also be able to explain the differences. Furthermore, they should be cautious about accusing countries such as Turkey, Russia, and Ethiopia of plotting to invade Israel when there is no evidence to support such a claim.

SIX

Babylon as the Symbol of Evil?

This chapter grapples with two prophetic Old Testament books that deal with ancient Babylon from differing perspectives, one apparently positive (Daniel) and the other clearly negative (Zechariah). In the Book of Daniel, chapters 2 and 7 unveil the future of Israel in terms of her relationship with four major world empires, one of which is clearly Babylon. The identification of the other three empires, however, is important as well, for this identification, especially of the fourth kingdom, has implications for understanding the end-times and Babylon's role in the end-times. King Nebuchadnezzar and his Babylonian Empire is the first kingdom listed and the most glorious. Nebuchadnezzar is one of the Mesopotamian kings whom Saddam Hussein likes to identify with, calling himself "the new Nebuchadnezzar." In Daniel 3 and 4, however, some very unusual events occur that cause King Nebuchadnezzar to acknowledge and even to praise God. What are we to make of his "confession"?

In Zechariah 5, on the other hand, the portrayal of Babylonia is negative. In one of Zechariah's night visions, he associates the empire with iniquity and idolatry. Zechariah was one of the last Old Testament books written, and, in fact, by Zechariah's time, Babylonia had been destroyed. Can we assume, therefore, that as the Old Testament drew to a close, biblical writers viewed the Babylonian Empire as a symbol of evil and idolatry?

Daniel and Babylon

The Book of Daniel is set during the Babylonian exile of Judah (about 550 B.C.). It is permeated with the theological story of Israel; that is, it describes the history of Israel's sin before God, the subsequent judgment followed by exile and the hope for her restoration to the land. Thus, in Daniel 1, the author begins by recalling Israel's current exile in Babylonia. The story concludes thematically with several prophecies regarding the future restoration of the Jews to their native country. The stone (the messianic kingdom) crushes the empires of the world in Daniel 2; the kingdom of the heavenly Son of Man appears in Daniel 7; and the final forgiveness and renewal of Israel is portrayed in Daniel 9:24–27. All of these descriptions refer to the same reality, namely, the sovereign power of God and the coming deliverance of Israel.

In the context of God's sovereign power, Daniel 2 and 4 (along with chapter 7) present three positive glimpses of Nebuchadnezzar in particular and Babylonia in general. The following discussion focuses on those three moments, overshadowed though they are in the greater picture of the role of Babylonia in the Bible.

DANIEL'S KINGDOMS AND THE EUROPEAN UNION

Although Daniel 2 and 7 record two separate dreams (the dream of Nebuchadnezzar in chapter 2 and Daniel's dream in chapter 7), they deal with the same scenario: the unfolding in history of four powerful kingdoms, beginning with the Babylonian kingdom of Daniel's day. Two basic approaches are used to identify those four kingdoms. Many interpreters argue for the following:

Kingdom	Leader	Date
Babylonian	Nebuchadnezzar	ca. 585 B.C.
Medo-Persian	Cyrus	ca. 539 B.C.
Greek	Alexander the Great	ca. 330 B.C.
Revived Roman Empire	Antichrist	In the end-time

The prediction of a revived Roman Empire is based largely on the identification of the fourth kingdom in Daniel 2 and 7. While this interpretation is certainly plausible, it is by no means certain, and there is no consensus among biblical scholars today regarding the identities of the kingdoms. Indeed, many scholars, evangelical and non-evangelical alike, associate the fourth kingdom with Alexander the Great. This understanding is presented below:

Kingdom	Leader	Date
Babylonian	Nebuchadnezzar	ca. 585 B.C.
Median	Astyages	ca. 550 B.C.
Persian	Cyrus	ca. 539 B.C.
Greek	Alexander the Great	ca. 330 B.C.

According to this reading, the fourth kingdom is Greece, not a revived Roman Empire. This kingdom has already existed in history, and therefore, an exclusively futuristic interpretation is not necessary. In other words, if the fourth kingdom is Alexander's Greek empire, then the modern-day doomsday equation of a revived Roman Empire (ruled by the Antichrist) and built on the European Common Market (i.e., the European Union) is not scriptural.

Over the past thirty years or so, many writers of books on biblical prophecy have viewed developments in Europe as steps toward the fulfillment of Daniel's prophecies. How do they make this connection? Daniel 7:7 reads, "I looked, and there before me was a fourth beast. . . . It was different from all the former beasts, and it had ten horns." Many popular prophecy writers such as Hal Lindsey have assumed (1) that the beast refers to a revived Roman Empire, (2) that Europe is the new embodiment of that empire, (3) that the ten horns refer to nations, and (4) that these must be European nations. Many of these writers have pointed to the European Union (often referred to as the European Common Market in earlier literature) as proof that this interpretation is correct. Is this valid?

In 1973, the European Union had nine members (Belgium, Germany, France, Italy, Luxembourg, the Netherlands, Denmark, Ireland, and the United Kingdom) and appeared to be close to fulfilling the ten-nation coalition portrayed in Daniel 7. In 1981, Greece joined the European Union, bringing the number to ten! Many popular doomsday writers of the 1970s and 1980s believed that the ten-member European Union was proof that the events of the end-times were under way and that the revived Roman Empire would emerge from this union. In 1981, this argument was rather convincing, and numerous writers confidently proclaimed that we were rapidly heading into the end-times. However, time passed. The end did not come. Instead, in 1986, two more countries (Spain and Portugal) joined the union. The EU now had twelve members. Then in 1995, three more countries joined (Austria, Finland, and Sweden), and the membership swelled to fifteen, where it technically remains today. However, on December 18, 2002, the EU voted to accept ten additional countries (Cyprus, the Czech Republic, Estonia, Hungary, Latvia, Lithuania, Malta, Poland, the Slovak Republic, and Slovenia), with their full membership to begin on May 1, 2004. Thus, in 2004, the membership will stand at twenty-five members. Therefore, the argument that the European Union was a fulfillment of the prophecy of Daniel 7 and signaled the rise of a ten-member revived Roman Empire has proven to be misleading. Clearly, the fifteen-member European Union (or the coming twenty-five-member Union) hardly fulfills the prophecy about a ten-horned beast.

Some writers such as Charles Dyer have acknowledged that the EU can no longer fulfill the *specifics* of the ten-member aspect of Daniel's prophecy. Yet Dyer still believes that Daniel refers to a European coalition, and he still argues that the European unity expressed in the EU reveals that we are near the end-times. Referring to the EU as the EEC, he writes:

> The goals of the EEC coincide with the Bible's predictions of an end-time power centered in Europe. A unified Europe—the economic and military powerhouse of the

81

world—looms just over the horizon. All that is lacking is a strong personality to galvanize and unify the various factions on the continent. And that person is coming![1]

What is puzzling is the assumption made by many writers that Europe is the equivalent of a revived Roman Empire. For sure, Italy, the country that contains Rome and the home country of the Roman Empire, is in Europe. But Dyer and the other writers do not talk much about Italy or even Rome itself (as the Protestant Reformers did in the sixteenth century, when they argued that the pope in Rome was the Antichrist). Therefore, it might be a good idea to look at the actual limits of the ancient Roman Empire. How European was it? How do the rest of the countries of the EU today line up with the Roman Empire of the first century A.D.? That is, do the countries in this peaceful European economic union of today resemble the ancient Roman Empire?

In the first century A.D., the Roman Empire consisted of territories that now comprise the modern countries of Italy, France, Spain, Portugal, Belgium, Luxemburg, England, Switzerland, Greece, Macedonia, Albania, Yugoslavia, Bosnia and Herzegovina, Serbia, Croatia, Slovenia, Austria, Romania, Bulgaria, Hungary, Turkey, Syria, Lebanon, Israel, Jordan, Egypt, and the coastal areas of Libya, Tunisia, Algeria, and Morocco. A very small portion of Germany, only the part that extends south of the Rhine, was also part of the Roman Empire.[2]

How does the EU compare? First of all, numerous countries now in the EU or accepted as new members in the EU were not part of the Roman Empire in the first century (and most of them never were in the Roman

Empire). These countries include most of Germany, most of the Netherlands, Denmark, Ireland, Finland, Sweden, the Czech Republic, Estonia, Latvia, Lithuania, Poland, and the Slovak Republic. Furthermore, extensive tracks of territory that were critical parts of the Roman Empire in the first century A.D. are not part of Europe and are not part of the EU. These countries (such as Egypt and Libya) were much more important to the economic health of Rome (they provided most of the food) than some of the fringe provinces such as Britain. Other countries that were part of the Roman Empire but are not connected to Europe or the European Union include Morocco, Algeria, Tunisia, Israel, Jordan, Lebanon, Syria, and Turkey (although Turkey has applied for membership in the EU). It is simply historically and geographically incorrect to assume that Europe is a modern-day Roman Empire.

So, first of all, a future revived Roman Empire is not mentioned explicitly in Scripture. Perhaps it is a possibility, but it is hardly a certainty. Furthermore, the mass of territory that comprises the European Union does not resemble the territory of the Roman Empire. In addition, these European countries have united peacefully for the sake of improving their economic well-being. Is it right for Christian writers to claim, based on flimsy evidence, that this economic union is playing into the hands of Satan? Is it moral to accuse the Europeans of forming the evil end-time empire of the Antichrist?

Tim LaHaye and Jerry Jenkins have abandoned the European hypothesis and have proclaimed instead that the *United Nations* will fulfill the ten-horned-beast prophecy of Daniel. They suggest that ten administrative regions of a United Nations–led world government are coming soon to fulfill Daniel's prophecy. However, it looks as if LaHaye and Jenkins occasionally tend to blur the distinction between current geopolitical fact and "Robert Ludlum style" imaginary fiction. LaHaye and Jenkins write, "Already there is almost universal acceptance among elite insiders that the governments of the world will relinquish their sovereignty to one head, an international world leader."[3] But LaHaye and Jenkins do not cite any sources to verify this claim. Who are these "elite insiders"? And if this view has found "universal acceptance," why has no one other than LaHaye and Jenkins ever heard of it? This statement may make sense in a Robert Ludlum novel, in which worldwide conspiracies are foundational to the plot, but in today's real world, it is nonsense. In fact, the trend in the world today is in the opposite direction—not toward larger, more centralized government entities but toward smaller, ethnic-specific government entities.[4] Unfortunately, thousands of well-intentioned Christians in America look to LaHaye as a leader in prophetic interpretation and thus often uncritically accept whatever he writes. How can he continue to make dogmatic statements about current geopolitical situations that are obviously incorrect?

Let's return to Daniel. Concerning the identification of the first kingdom in Daniel 2 and 7 there is no debate. The head of the statue made of fine gold, the most valuable of metals (Dan. 2:32, 37–38), and the lion with the wings of an eagle, an ancient symbol for Babylon (Dan. 7:4), represent the Babylonian kingdom under King Nebuchadnezzar. Nebuchadnezzar's empire was superior to the other kingdoms because God deemed it so:

You, O king, are the king of kings. The God of heaven has given you dominion and power and might and glory; in your hands he has placed mankind and the beasts of the field and the birds of the air. Wherever they live, he has made you ruler over them all. You are that head of gold.

Daniel 2:37–38

Surprisingly, Daniel 2:46–48 reveals that Nebuchadnezzar reacts to Daniel's interpretation of the dream by praising God and exalting Daniel:

Then King Nebuchadnezzar fell prostrate before Daniel and paid him honor and ordered that an offering and incense be presented to him. The king said to Daniel, "Surely your God is the God of gods and the Lord of kings and a revealer of mysteries, for you were able to reveal this mystery." Then the king placed Daniel in a high position and lavished many gifts on him. He made him ruler over the entire province of Babylon and placed him in charge of all its wise men.

These are indeed positive remarks about Nebuchadnezzar and his empire. It is also interesting to note that Nebuchadnezzar and Babylon are not connected in any way to Daniel's prophecy of a ten-horned beast. There is no hint in Daniel that Babylon will be rebuilt and will become the capital of a ten-nation world government, supposedly depicted by this beast. This silence is significant and further erodes the position that Babylon will be rebuilt in the end-times to become the capital of either a European or a United Nations empire led by the Antichrist.

THE FIERY FURNACE

The episode of the three men in the fiery furnace is well known among Christians around the world. The story begins with King Nebuchadnezzar setting up a colossal statue of himself for the purpose of soliciting the worship of his people. Although all the Babylonians bow before the statue of Nebuchadnezzar, three Hebrew young men—Shadrach, Meshach, and Abednego—refuse to do so. They are determined to worship the God of Israel alone, even though they are in captivity in Babylonia and are under the political power of the Babylonians. Nebuchadnezzar gives them the opportunity to recant, but they do not. Consequently, the Babylonian king fires up one of his furnaces seven times its normal temperature and orders the soldiers to throw the three Hebrews into the furnace. In the process, the soldiers are burned alive by the extreme heat.

Yet when King Nebuchadnezzar looks into the furnace, he sees not only that the men are not incinerated but also that there are four, not three, individuals in the furnace. He says, "Look! I see four men walking around in the fire, unbound and unharmed, and the fourth looks like a son of the gods" (Dan. 3:25). When the three men are removed from the oven, not a hair on their heads has been singed. Then in a dramatic turn of events, the king praises the faith of the three men as well as their God:

> Then Nebuchadnezzar said, "Praise be to the God of Shadrach, Meshach and Abednego, who has sent his angel and rescued his servants! They trusted in him and defied the king's command and were willing to give up their lives rather than serve or worship any god except their own

God. Therefore I decree that the people of any nation or language who say anything against the God of Shadrach, Meshach and Abednego be cut into pieces and their houses be turned into piles of rubble, for no other god can save in this way." Then the king promoted Shadrach, Meshach and Abednego in the province of Babylon.

Daniel 3:28–30

One of the ironic theological truths presented in this story is that Nebuchadnezzar, the Babylonian king who had recently killed thousands of Hebrews and burned Jerusalem to the ground, is not able to kill these three young Hebrews right in his own backyard. God had brought him to power and indeed had used him as an agent of judgment against Judah and Jerusalem. Now, however, in the case of the three young men, Nebuchadnezzar is at odds with God and thus powerless to strike down these defiant Hebrews, even in his capital city of Babylon.

At any rate, Nebuchadnezzar's statements are startling. Does he now believe in only one God—the God of the Hebrews? Or is he asserting only that the God of Israel is superior among all the other gods he acknowledges? The answer is not clear. Nonetheless, there is no doubt that the Babylonian king praises God and is thereby blessed by God. This story does not present Nebuchadnezzar as an antagonist and a prototypical enemy of God, at least not at the end of the story. It shows Nebuchadnezzar acknowledging the power of God.

THE BABYLONIAN KING PRAISES GOD AGAIN

Daniel 4 records another enigmatic dream of Nebuchadnezzar, one that only Daniel could decipher. The

87

dream is about an enormous, fruitful tree. But no sooner does it touch the sky than a messenger from heaven cuts it down and strips its branches! Curiously, however, the stump and roots of the fallen tree remain. Then, suddenly, the stump is addressed as though it were a man:

> Let him be drenched with the dew of heaven, and let him live with the animals among the plants of the earth. Let his mind be changed from that of a man and let him be given the mind of an animal, till seven times pass by for him.

Daniel 4:15b–16

The point of the dream is then declared:

> The decision is announced by messengers, the holy ones declare the verdict, so that the living may know that the Most High is sovereign over the kingdoms of men and gives them to anyone he wishes and sets over them the lowliest of men.

Daniel 4:17

Daniel then gives his interpretation of the dream. At the height of Nebuchadnezzar's reign, God will humble the great Babylonian king by causing him to become insane, even to the point of living like an animal. Sure enough, a year later the dream is fulfilled. While Nebuchadnezzar pridefully gazes over Babylon, he is struck down with insanity, an insanity that lasts for seven years. However, at the end of that time, the king repents of his arrogance, and God restores his sanity and his kingdom.

As a result, Nebuchadnezzar again worships the God of Israel:

> At the end of that time, I, Nebuchadnezzar, raised my eyes toward heaven, and my sanity was restored. Then I praised the Most High; I honored and glorified him who lives forever. His dominion is an eternal dominion; his kingdom endures from generation to generation. All the peoples of the earth are regarded as nothing. He does as he pleases with the powers of heaven and the peoples of the earth. No one can hold back his hand or say to him: "What have you done?" At the same time that my sanity was restored, my honor and splendor were returned to me for the glory of my kingdom. My advisers and nobles sought me out, and I was restored to my throne and became even greater than before. Now I, Nebuchadnezzar, praise and exalt and glorify the King of heaven, because everything he does is right and all his ways are just. And those who walk in pride he is able to humble.
>
> Daniel 4:34–37

Once again, the Book of Daniel presents Nebuchadnezzar as one who acknowledges and praises the God of Israel. The interpretive approach that sees Nebuchadnezzar as the prototype of end-time evil is not consistent with Daniel's positive remarks about this ancient Babylonian king.

In light of the above discussion, the connection between Nebuchadnezzar and Saddam Hussein is not a close one. It is also important to note that none of the passages about Nebuchadnezzar mentions that the city of Babylon needs to be rebuilt to be destroyed again. These passages in Daniel not only underscore the power of God over forces hostile to his people but also demonstrate that often God's most powerful enemies are brought to the point of acknowledging his power and sovereignty. The lesson of Nebuchadnezzar is also one of hope, for if this terrible Babylonian king can see the power of God and repent, then there is hope for other hostile political leaders, even someone as twisted as Saddam Hussein.

The Woman in the Basket Goes to Babylon

The prophet Zechariah was born during the Babylonian exile and was one of the Jews who returned to Judah in 538 B.C. after Cyrus the Persian defeated Babylon and allowed the Jewish captives to return to their homeland. The Book of Zechariah dates to roughly 520 B.C., and its main message is similar to that of Daniel and the other prophets before him: the story of Israel as portrayed through the themes of sin, exile, and restoration. Indeed, the opening words of the book speak of Israel's past sin (1:2), her rejection of the prophets' call for repentance (1:4), the resulting exile in Babylonia (1:4b–6a; 12), and the actualization of the hope for restoration (1:3, 6b).

Zechariah 1–8 records eight night visions communicated to the prophet by God. Babylon appears in Zechariah 5, in which the prophet relates a rather humorous account of God's act of cleansing his restored people of wickedness and idolatry. Zechariah 5:5–11 records the fascinating seventh vision of the woman in a basket. The passage reads:

Then the angel who was speaking to me came forward and said to me, "Look up and see what this is that is appearing." I asked, "What is it?" He replied, "It is a measuring basket." And he added, "This is the iniquity of the people throughout the land." Then the cover of lead was raised, and there in the basket sat a woman! He said, "This is wickedness," and he pushed her back into the basket and pushed the lead cover down over its mouth. Then I looked up—and there before me were two women, with the wind in their wings! They had wings like those of a stork, and they lifted up the basket between heaven and earth. "Where are they taking the basket?" I asked the angel who was speaking to me. He replied, "To the country of Babylonia to build a house for it. When it is ready, the basket will be set there in its place."

This measuring basket (an *ephah*) was apparently larger than normal, and it symbolized the iniquity of Israel. When the cover of the basket was raised, out came not grain but a woman! The shock such a scene caused might be compared to a woman popping out of a cake at a modern-day bachelor's party. The angel guiding Zechariah, however, declares that this woman is "iniquity," and he shoves her back into the basket and replaces the lead cover. Then two other women with wings, apparently angels, take the basket and airfreight it to Babylonia, apparently the appropriate place to send iniquity.[5] The woman in the basket also probably represents idolatry, the specific wickedness of Israel that is being addressed.[6]

Obviously, there is a serious point behind this funny story. As God restores his people, he cleanses them of iniquity and idolatry, removing it from their midst and sending it away. Where does he send this symbolic basket filled with iniquity? To Babylonia. What better place than the region that epitomized rebellion against God, as the tower of Babel story in Genesis 11 illustrated? What better place than the land of the Babylonians, who had devastated Jerusalem because of her idolatry and to which she had been exiled after her punishment by God? Zechariah does not appear to be referring to the literal empire of Babylon. By the time of Zechariah's vision, the Persians had already brought an end to the Babylonian Empire. Thus, Zechariah uses Babylon as the symbol of an evil place characterized by iniquity and idolatry.

By the end of the Old Testament, therefore, at least by the time of the writing of Zechariah, Babylonia had apparently become a symbol for evil. This reality was not lost on the apostle John, who in Revelation 17–18 describes Babylon as an evil woman who tempts the people of God to sin. The NIV Study Bible well summarizes the significance of Zechariah's "woman in the basket" vision by stating, "Babylonia, a land of idolatry, was an appropriate locale for wickedness—but not Israel, where God chose to dwell with his people. Only after purging it of its evil would the Promised Land truly be the 'Holy Land' (Zech. 2:12)."

Conclusion

This chapter was devoted to a discussion of Daniel and Zechariah, especially to their respectively positive and negative statements about ancient Babylonia, but also to the identification of Daniel's fourth beast and its relationship to modern Europe. An analysis of

Daniel's message revealed some amazingly complimentary remarks about Nebuchadnezzar's budding faith in Israel's God. Any comparisons, therefore, between Nebuchadnezzar and Saddam Hussein are probably misguided. Saddam has more in common with the Soviet tyrant Joseph Stalin than he does with Nebuchadnezzar.[7] Zechariah, however, speaks only of ancient Babylonia and not of Nebuchadnezzar. The visions recorded by Zechariah, especially that of the woman in the basket (Zech. 5:5–11), vilify Babylonia as the epitome of iniquity and evil. By the end of the Old Testament, therefore, Babylon has become the symbol of iniquity. The infamous leader of Babylon, however, illustrates the power of God to bring pagan, idolatrous rulers to repentance and an acknowledgment of him.

This chapter also questioned whether Daniel's fourth beast does indeed refer to a revived Roman Empire. Stark differences between the ancient Roman Empire and the modern European Union were underscored, highlighting the fact that events in contemporary Europe seem to have little if any connection to Daniel's vision of a ten-horned beast.

The next chapter suggests that the New Testament writers view Babylonia symbolically, as did Zechariah. Indeed, Revelation 17–18 depicts evil as a woman in Babylon. But are we to understand that person as a revived end-time empire headed by Saddam Hussein? That is the question to which we now turn.

SEVEN

Rome and the Rise of Babylon in the Book of Revelation

—

"The evil one." "A member of the evil axis." "A builder of weapons of mass destruction." President George W. Bush has used these strong descriptive labels in reference to Iraqi strongman Saddam Hussein. Saddam's reign of terror has been marked by the murder of his rivals, the use of chemical warfare against his own people, support of international terrorism, and open hatred of Israel and the United States.

One would think that the defeat of Saddam's forces in the Gulf War, the United Nations' sanctions against Iraq, the no-fly zones imposed on his military, and the general scorn of Arab nations would have silenced this boastful despot. But Saddam's bellicose taunts and delusions of grandeur have persisted, to the irritation of the United States and the Western world.

Since September 11, 2001, the American government and its citizens have intensified their nervous watch over Iraq as concerns have mounted that Saddam is moving full-speed toward developing weapons of mass destruction, particularly nuclear weapons. If Saddam can develop nuclear bombs and place them in the hands of fanatical terrorists, he would be able to inflict damage on the free world that could make September 11 pale in comparison. Indeed, on September 8, 2002, United States Defense Secretary Donald Rumsfeld stated this fear succinctly on *Face the Nation:* "Imagine a September 11 with weapons of mass destruction. It's not 3,000; it's tens of thousands of innocent men, women, and children."[1]

Given these real circumstances, it does not take much imagination to envision a scenario in which Iraq's actions could spark cataclysmic events in the world, such as the detonation of nuclear weapons in Western cities or even open war between Muslim countries and Western democracies. Those who believe Iraq will rise again in the end-times take every opportunity to appeal to Scripture for support of such a possibility. Indeed, they argue that the possibility of such a scenario indicates we are presently moving into the apocalyptic end-times.

In chapter 4, we saw that the preceding theory is not correct in light of Old Testament prophecies concerning the fall of Babylon. Babylon has fallen for good. But what about Revelation 17–18? Perhaps those chapters envision a future end-time role for Babylon. The following remarks evaluate that hypothesis.

Will a Modern Iraqi City of Babylon Rise from the Ashes?

In the Bible, Revelation 18:10 states, "Woe! Woe, O great city, O Babylon, city of power! In one hour your doom has come!" Doesn't this text (and the rest of Revelation 17 and 18) teach that a literal Babylon *must* be resurrected to play a critical role in the end-times?

Several popular writers assert that Revelation 17–18 predicts the return of a literal Babylon in the end-times. They argue that Babylon will be the city that will be destroyed by Christ himself at his second coming. Charles Dyer, for example, writes, "Every day that passes brings us closer to the end-times, and every day the eyes of the world focus more closely on events in the Middle East and Mesopotamia. One key element in God's program of end-time activities will be the reestablishment of Babylon as a world power."[2] But what is the evidence for such a claim? The advocates of a resurrected Babylon theory present three arguments to support this view.

SADDAM WANTS TO REBUILD BABYLON

The first argument relates to current events—the rather recent political scene in the Middle East.[3] During the last decade of the twentieth century, and thanks to the efforts of Saddam Hussein, Babylon has once again attracted worldwide attention. Thus, the October 11, 1990, edition of the *New York Times International* could state:

Under President Saddam Hussein one of the ancient world's most legendary cities has begun to rise again.

97

More than an archaeological venture, the new Babylon is self-consciously dedicated to the idea that Nebuchadnezzar has a successor in Mr. Hussein, whose military prowess and vision will restore to Iraqis the glory their ancestors knew when all of what is now Iraq, Syria, Lebanon, Jordan, Kuwait, and Israel was under Babylonian control.[4]

Paul Lewis in the *San Francisco Chronicle* elaborated on the connection between Nebuchadnezzar and Saddam:

When King Nebuchadnezzar ran things around here some 2,500 years ago, he left clear instructions for the future kings of Babylon that are finally being carried out. Writing in cuneiform script on tablets of clay, the royal scribes urged their master's successors to repair and rebuild his temples and palaces. Today, in a gesture rich in political significance, President Saddam Hussein, Iraq's strong-armed ruler, is sparing no effort to obey that now-distant command.[5]

Saddam's dreams and plans of rebuilding Babylon certainly do not symbolize peace. Begun at the height of the Iraq-Iran war (1980 to 1988), the project to rebuild Babylon was a rallying point for the Iraqis' sinking morale during the war against Iran (ancient Persia). Thus, the Iraqi minister of information and culture, Latif Nsayyif Jassim, asserted:

The Persian (Iranian) mentality in our neighborhood, prompted by deep-rooted hatred and aggressiveness, tried to quench the flame of civilization in this city of Babylon. Hence the city came under the attack of the Persian ruler Kurash [Cyrus] who, before 2,500 years, laid siege to this town. The siege lasted long and the town remained strong. It was not until Cyrus had collaborated with the Jews inside the city that he was able to tighten the siege round the city and subsequently to occupy it. . . . Today we are living in the midst of Khomeini's aggression which has extended over a span of seven years during which Khomeini had allied himself with the Zionists in an attempt to enter Baghdad and other Iraqi cities and destroy them as was the case with Babylon. . . . It [a rebuilt Babylon] will serve as a living example of the grandeur of the Iraqis to pursue their path for more glories.[6]

The Babylon renewal project was associated with more than an Iraqi victory over Iran. It also symbolized Saddam's desire to control the Persian Gulf (which, together with Saudi Arabia, Kuwait, and Iraq, constitutes one-half of the world's oil supply) as well as "the Arab world, where he aspires to hegemony, to being the single most important leader. . . . He sees himself as Nasser's heir in the Arab world."[7]

Even Saddam's loss in the 1991 Gulf War did not dampen his efforts at rebuilding Babylon. In September 1992, Iraq sent out invitations for the Fourth International Babylon Festival. Guests from around the world were encouraged to gaze on the city's reconstruction:

Work is underway on a series of three huge viewing platforms just outside the walls of Nebuchadnezzar's Babylon from which visitors will be able to look down at new excavations Iraq is planning. "This is the personal orders of the President," said Iraq's Director General of Antiquities, Mouyad Said.[8]

Clearly, Saddam Hussein has big dreams of rebuilding the ancient Babylonian Empire. But is this the fulfillment of prophecy? Does it signal the imminence of the end-time apocalyptic wars? These are serious conclusions with profound ramifications. We need to be absolutely sure that these conclusions are based on a true interpretation of Scripture and not merely on speculation and current events.

OLD TESTAMENT PROPHECY MUST BE FULFILLED

The second line of argumentation used to support the view that Babylon will rise again in the end-times is based on Old Testament prophecies that forecast Babylon's destruction (Isa. 13:1–6; Jer. 14:1–4, 7; 50–51). According to this reasoning, because ancient Babylon was never fully annihilated, as these prophecies predict, the literal fulfillment of these prophecies must lie in the future. Thus, these prophecies must apply to a future, modern-day, resurrected Babylon. This argument, however, was refuted in chapter 4, which demonstrated clearly that the destruction of ancient Babylon did indeed fulfill these prophecies.

THE GREAT HARLOT OF REVELATION 17–18 REPRESENTS THE MODERN CITY OF BABYLON

The third and most important argument is that Revelation 17–18 predicts that Babylon will rise again as a sign of the end-times. In these two fascinating chapters, the apostle John portrays the nemesis of God's kingdom as a harlot dressed in scarlet and riding on a beast. She is covered with blasphemous names and rules over the kings of the earth in opposition to God. Those who argue for the resurrection of Babylon identify this harlot with the literal city of Babylon for three reasons.

First, the city the harlot represents is actually called Babylon (Rev. 17:4–6; cf. 14:8; 16:19). Robert Thomas writes of this:

> John used city names in Revelation 1–3, all in a nonfigurative sense. When he does use a city name figuratively, he makes that clear (see 11:8). The best solution is faithfulness to literal interpretation—that is, identifying Babylon as the city on the Euphrates River. In fact, Revelation mentions that river twice, both times in a literal sense (9:14; 16:12). The imposing influence of that city and its dominance in world affairs are major considerations during the time period just before Christ returns to judge her. Literal Babylon's visibility may be minimal at a given time in history, but the city could rise to world prominence very quickly.[9]

Second, Babylon is said to sit on many waters (17:1), which recalls the moat that surrounded the ancient city. In addition, the Euphrates River flowed through the middle of the ancient city, and the encompassing region was crisscrossed with canals and irrigation ditches.

Third, as cited above, the case for a literal reading of Babylon is strengthened by an actual reference to the Euphrates River in Revelation 16:12 (cf. 17:1). Because ancient Babylon lay on the banks of the Euphrates, some people believe this reference makes a clear connection with Babylon.

Why Don't New Testament Scholars Believe This?

These arguments appear to be quite convincing. Indeed, they are fueling the popular view that the Iraqis need to resurrect the city of Babylon. Adherents of this view then expect this modern city of Babylon to play a central role in the end-times, as depicted in the Book of Revelation. Is this true? Does Saddam's hope to rebuild Babylon signal the inauguration of the end-times of Revelation?

On the other hand, if this argument for a literal, future, resurrected city of Babylon is so strong, why does a majority of New Testament scholars reject it? This view persists only in popular literature; it is practically absent from scholarly literature on the Book of Revelation. This situation, of course, does not in and of itself disprove the view. After all, we are concerned with what the Bible actually teaches, not just with what scholars say. But in popular literature, views can be stated without having to withstand serious, biblically based, scholarly scrutiny; therefore, the "resurrected modern city of Babylon" view goes largely unchallenged. In scholarly literature, however, this view has been rigorously challenged on biblical grounds and has been found wanting. The discussion that follows attempts to present the biblical and historical rebuttal to the resurrected Babylon theory and to explain the view that is supported by most New Testament scholarship.

The Harlot of Revelation 17–18 Symbolizes Ancient Rome and Not Modern Babylon

Most commentators rightly identify Babylon in Revelation 17–18 with the Rome of John's day. Several pieces of evidence support such a view.

THE BOOK OF REVELATION USES SYMBOLIC LANGUAGE

First, the Book of Revelation is filled with symbolic, figurative language. Both views maintain that the harlot of Revelation 17–18 symbolizes a city. The beast is symbolic as well. The extensive use of symbolism and figurative language by the apostle John to convey specific truth statements at least opens the door to the possibility that the term *Babylon* may be symbolic as well. In fact, since practically all the other terms in Revelation 17–18 are seen as symbols (harlot, beast, horns, etc.), understanding the term *Babylon* in a symbolic sense would reflect a more consistent interpretation of this passage than that of interpreting this term alone as a literal reference.

ROME HAS SEVEN HILLS AND BABYLON DOES NOT

If the term *Babylon* is used symbolically, then it probably refers to the first-century city of Rome rather than to a resurrected, modern-day city of Babylon. Indeed, Revelation 17–18 makes numerous connections between the city it calls Babylon and the ancient city of Rome. First of all, Revelation 17:9 portrays the great harlot and the beast as seated on seven hills. The ancient city of Rome was comprised of seven hills; indeed, it was famous for these hills. The literature of the ancient world contains dozens of references and descriptions of the seven hills of Rome. We even know their names: Capitol, Aventine, Caelin, Esquiline, Quirinal, Viminal, and Palestine.[10] On the other hand, one looks in vain for an association of Babylon with seven hills. No such description was ever used of Babylon.

ROMAN COINS AND JOHN'S IMAGE OF THE HARLOT

Another important key for identifying the harlot and the beast of Revelation 17–18 as ancient Rome instead of modern Babylon is found on a coin minted in A.D. 71 in Asia Minor (the home of the seven churches mentioned in Revelation 2–3) during the reign of the Roman emperor Vespasian (A.D. 69–79). This coin is known as the *Dea Roma* Coin.

The *Dea Roma* Coin (minted A.D. 71). This coin is on exhibit in the British Museum in London.

One side of the coin contains a portrait of the emperor with the Latin inscription IMP CAESAR VESPASIANVS AVG PM TP PP COS III, standard abbreviations for "Emperor Caesar Vespasian Augustus, Pontifex Maximus [Greatest Priest], Tribunicia Potestas [Tribunal Power], Pater Patiae [Father of the Fatherland], Consul for the Third Time."[11]

The reverse side of the coin depicts Roma, a pagan goddess of Rome, sitting on seven hills. This image of a woman sitting on seven hills was obviously a way of representing Rome in the symbolic art of the day that would have been recognized by people of this time period. John's readers would certainly have understood it that way. The goddess Roma wears military dress, and a small sword in her left hand rests on her left knee, symbolizing the military might of Rome. She is flanked on the left and the right by the letters S and C, which stand for *senatus consultum* (a resolution of the Senate). The river god Tiber reclines against the seven hills at the right. A group consisting of a miniature she-wolf with the twins Romulus and Remus suckling is located on the left side.

Some experts believe that Revelation 17 may actually be a detailed description of this particular coin. In other words, John's vision of Babylon in Revelation is based on the *Dea Roma* Coin, suggesting an ironic and not-so-subtle criticism of Rome and all that Rome represents. The resemblances between the two are indeed striking:

1. The goddess Roma, the deity who represented and protected Rome, sits on the seven hills of that city. The harlot of Revelation likewise sits on seven hills (Rev. 17:9).
2. In some of the Roman legends, the she-wolf who nurses Romulus and Remus carried the connotation of a harlot. The woman in Revelation 17–18 is likewise called a harlot.
3. On the coin the woman is seated by the waters of the Tiber River. The harlot in Revelation sits "on many waters" (17:1, 15).
4. There is a possible connection between the phrase "Mystery, Babylon the Great, the Mother of Prostitutes" (17:5) and the label *Roma* on the

coin. The city of Rome was itself regarded to be a deity with a concealed name. Yet that "secret" name was widely thought by many Romans to be Amor (the goddess of love and sexuality), which is Roma spelled backward. When John describes the goddess sitting on the seven hills but then calls her the mother of prostitutes, he seems to be consciously dragging the popular matron deity of Rome and even Rome itself down into the dirt. His portrayal is a harsh, critical parody.

5. The vision of Revelation 17 presents the woman as drunk with the blood of the saints who are witnesses of Jesus (17:6). This may be depicted by Roma holding the Roman sword, which represented the power of Rome. At the time John wrote the Book of Revelation, the Roman imperial worship system was persecuting and executing Christians. The *Dea Roma* Coin equates Caesar Vespasian (the obverse side) with Roma (the reverse side) and thereby provides John with the basis to identify the harlot of Rome with the imperial cult. This is so because the Roman emperor Augustus (31 B.C.–A.D. 14) initiated the custom of building temples dedicated to both caesar and Roma (the personification of Rome). Augustus commissioned the building of four temples in honor of himself and Roma, two in Asia (Pergamon and Ephesus) and two in Bithynia (Nicea and Nicomedia). Thereafter, coins portraying the emperor on one side and Roma on the other side indicated that the two went hand in hand in implementing caesar worship.

This final point has devastating consequences for the popular view (held by Dyer and others) that the beast of Revelation 17 is a future Antichrist ruling a European Union dominated by Iraq's oil industry. If the *Dea Roma* Coin is indeed the basis for John's vision in Revelation 17, then the beast (caesar) and the harlot (Roma) are one and the same—ancient Rome!

THE LUXURY AND WEALTH OF ANCIENT ROME

In addition, the luxury of Babylon portrayed in Revelation 18:11–13 matches descriptions of ancient Rome's wealth and role in world trade. This fascinating passage reads as follows:

> The merchants of the earth will weep and mourn over her because no one buys their cargoes any more—cargoes of gold, silver, precious stones and pearls; fine linen, purple, silk and scarlet cloth; every sort of citron wood, and articles of every kind made of ivory, costly wood, bronze, iron and marble; cargoes of cinnamon and spice, of incense, myrrh and frankincense, of wine and olive oil, of fine flour and wheat; cattle and sheep; horses and carriages; and bodies and souls of men.

The terminology used by John is precisely the same type of language used in the first century to describe Rome. In a first-century description by a Roman writer known as Pliny the Elder, thirteen elements of commercial wealth cited in Revelation 18:11–13 are repeated. The similarity is telling:

> The most costly product of the sea is the *pearl;* of the earth's surface, rock-crystal; of the earth's interior, *dia-*

107

monds, emeralds, gemstones [Revelation uses the generic expression "precious stones"] and vessels of fluor-spar of the earth's increase, the scarlet kermes-insect and silphium, with spikenard and *silks* from leaves, *citrus wood*, balsam, *myrrh* and *frankincense*, which exude from trees or shrubs, and costus from roots. As for animals . . . the most costly product found on land is the *elephant's tusk* [ivory], and on sea the turtle's shell. Of the hides and coats of animals, the most costly are the pelts dyed in China and the Arabian she-goat's tufted beard which we call "ladanum." Of creatures that belong to both land and sea, the most costly products are *scarlet* and *purple* dyes made from shell-fish. . . . We must not forget to mention that *gold* for which all mankind has so mad a passion, comes scarcely tenth in the list of valuables, while *silver*, with which we purchase gold, is almost as low as twentieth.[12]

The Apostle Peter Uses Babylon as a Code for Rome

The use of Babylon as a "code" or symbol for Rome is not restricted to the Book of Revelation. The apostle Peter uses the same term to refer to Rome at the end of his first epistle. He writes, "She who is in Babylon, chosen together with you, sends you her greetings, and so does my son Mark" (1 Peter 5:13). Neither Peter nor Mark is ever associated with the literal city of Babylon. Nowhere in Scripture or in early Christian writings is there a reference to Peter or Mark visiting Babylon. However, Scripture does describe Peter's ministry as moving northward from Palestine to Syrian Antioch (Gal. 2:11) and then westward to Corinth (1 Cor. 1:12) in the direction of Rome. Scripture also places both Peter and Mark in Rome at the end of Peter's ministry (cf. 1 Peter 5:13 with Col. 4:10; Philem. 23–24). The consensus of New Testament scholarship is that Peter is referring to the church when he says "she" and that "Babylon" is a coded reference to Rome.

NON-BIBLICAL JEWISH WRITINGS USE BABYLON AS A CODE FOR ROME

Several Jewish literary works date from the first century A.D. These texts are not inspired, and therefore Christians do not use them for doctrine or Christian guidance. However, they are helpful in providing historical background for the New Testament and shedding light on terms and phrases used in the New Testament. One such document, the *Sibylline Oracles,* is commonly dated to the latter half of the first century, the same era in which John wrote the Book of Revelation. This ancient document uses Babylon as a code for Rome in much the same fashion as Peter does. However, the parallels between the *Sibylline Oracles* and Revelation 17–18 are more extensive than just a reference to Babylon. This document contains a prophecy against Rome that incorporates the following elements: (1) Rome is called Babylon; (2) Rome is portrayed as an immoral woman; and (3) this immoral woman sits by the banks of the Tiber River. Note that the references to Italy, the Latin land, and the River Tiber clearly identify the city as Rome. The text reads as follows:

> A great star will come from heaven to the wondrous
>   sea
> and will burn the deep sea and Babylon itself
> and the land of Italy, because of which many
> holy faithful Hebrews and a true people perished. . . .

With you are found adulteries. . . .
Alas, city of the Latin land, unclean in all things,
Rejoicing in vipers, as a widow you will sit
By the banks, and the River Tiber will weep for you,
    its consort.[13]

Several other non-biblical Jewish writings of the first century A.D. also use Babylon as a symbol for Rome.[14] Obviously, in first-century Jewish and Christian communities, Babylon was a fairly common symbol that was often used as a substitute term for the city of Rome. The apostle John wrote the Book of Revelation during this same time period. He—as well as his first-century readers—would have been very familiar with this usage of the term *Babylon*. In this context and against this background, we can be quite certain that in the Book of Revelation the apostle John used the term *Babylon* in a similar fashion—to represent Rome, not to refer to a resurrected Iraqi city in Mesopotamia.

Conclusion

The evidence is overwhelming. The term *Babylon* in the Book of Revelation does not refer to a future resurrected city in Iraq. It is used to refer to the first-century city of Rome. The evidence from Revelation 17–18 can be summarized as follows. The Book of Revelation uses symbols and imagery to convey the truth of its prophecy. If the harlot of Revelation 17–18 refers symbolically to a city—as all scholars agree—then we should not be surprised to find that the term *Babylon* is used symbolically as well. Next, in Revelation 17–18, the harlot called Babylon is portrayed as sitting on seven hills. This is a clear connection to Rome, which was built on seven hills and even issued coins depicting a goddess sitting on these hills. There is no connection between Babylon and seven hills. Further, the description of the city's wealth in Revelation 17–18 matches common descriptions of Rome from this era. In addition, authors of non-biblical Jewish literature of the first century often used Babylon as a symbol of Rome, thus indicating that this was a common literary connection. Finally, and quite significantly, the apostle Peter used the term *Babylon* to represent the ancient city of Rome in his letter 1 Peter. If biblical authors such as Peter used the term *Babylon* as a code for Rome, why shouldn't we accept this meaning when the apostle John uses the term?

The arguments of Dyer, LaHaye, and the other doomsday writers who predict the prophetic resurrection of Babylon simply do not hold water and do not stand up against close scrutiny of the biblical texts. The argument from Old Testament prophecy was refuted in chapter 4. Indeed, in contradiction to the modern resurrected Babylon theory, Jeremiah and the other prophets proclaimed that Babylon would *never* be resurrected after the Medes and Persians conquered it. The doomsday arguments from Revelation 17–18 have likewise been shown to be misinterpretations of the biblical text. All that is left, therefore, is Saddam's dream of rebuilding the Babylonian Empire, but this futile dream has no connection to biblical prophecy. There is absolutely no biblical evidence to support the theory that Babylon will be resurrected to play a role in the end-times.

The problem with the view of LaHaye, Dyer, and others is that it might very well have a damaging effect on American foreign policy. It is extremely dangerous for

111

Americans to think that large-scale war in the Middle East is an imminent prophetic certainty. And how disastrously foolish Americans are to hold this view when the biblical evidence in fact argues against it! The Bible does not forecast end-time prominence for Iraq, and it is important for interpreters of the Bible to realize this, for only then can they avoid the possible devastating results of misinterpreting Scripture. The tragic end of self-proclaimed prophets such as Jim Jones and David Koresh are ready reminders of the power of self-fulfilling prophecies. Even scarier is the global threat that could result from the wedding of contemporary misinformed biblical prophecy and American foreign policy in the Middle East. D. S. Russell, an expert on Jewish-Christian apocalyptic literature, expressed this point during the Cold War well over twenty years ago, and it bears repeating today:

> One rather frightening by-product of this process of interpretation is that it is so easy to *create* the very situation which is being described so that the interpretation given brings about its own fulfillment. Russia, for example, is to be destroyed by nuclear attack—and scripture must be fulfilled! It needs little imagination to understand the consequences of such a belief, especially if held with deep conviction by politicians and the military who have the power to press the button and to execute the judgment thus prophesied and foreordained.[15]

EIGHT

Nebuchadnezzar to Saddam and Beyond

On the back cover of Charles Dyer's book *The Rise of Babylon: Sign of the End Times* is a picture of a commemorative medallion with Saddam Hussein pictured next to the ancient king of Babylon, King Nebuchadnezzar. Next to the picture the book cover declares, "Saddam Hussein and the ancient world conqueror Nebuchadnezzar. Not only do they look alike, but their mission is the same—to control the world. And the symbol of this world dominion is an ancient city . . . BABYLON: Prelude to Armageddon?"

Without doubt, Saddam likes to compare himself to Nebuchadnezzar, among others. Is Dyer correct in being alarmed over the similarity between Saddam and Nebuchadnezzar? Does this "similarity" somehow signal the coming end-times? What is Saddam's actual ethnic connection to Nebuchadnezzar? What happened historically in Iraq between the fall of Nebuchadnezzar's Babylonian Empire in 539 B.C. and the rise of Saddam Hussein in the latter part of the twentieth century? Who lives in Iraq now? Are they Babylonians? If not, who are they and where did they come from?

Persians, Greeks, More Persians, and Christians

Chapter 2 briefly discussed the great ancient Mesopotamian civilizations that developed in the area now known as Iraq. As mentioned earlier, the Babylonian Empire that played such an important role in the Bible was overrun by Cyrus and the Persians in 539 B.C. Persia was the name of the ancient area to the east of Iraq now known as Iran. The ethnic term *Persian* is often used interchangeably with the term *Iranian*. These people were ethnically different from those in Mesopotamia, and during Persian rule, a certain amount of emigration from Persia to Mesopotamia occurred. Economically, the area that had comprised the former Babylonian Empire was neglected, and it declined substantially during Persian rule.

Alexander the Great swept through the area in 331 B.C., defeating the Persians and bringing Greek cultural influence to the region. Alexander had extensive plans for redeveloping Babylon and the Babylonian region, but he died shortly after his conquest. His empire quickly split into several sections as each of his generals fought for a piece of the pie he had left behind. Mesopotamia fell under the control of the Seleucid dynasty, but by 163 B.C. they had lost control of the area.

For the next few hundred years, Iraq was a battleground between the Romans and the Parthians, who had by this time conquered Iran (Persia). Large numbers of Persians from the east moved into the region during these years. However, in A.D. 224, an indigenous tribal monarchy in Iran called the Sassanids wrested Iran and Mesopotamia (Iraq) from the Parthians. The Sassanids then controlled Mesopotamia for approximately four hundred years. During that time they introduced the Zoroastrian religion into the region, but it met with only limited success, for Christianity was also penetrating Mesopotamia from the west. When the Sassanid rulers were pushed out of Iraq by the Arabs at the end of the sixth century A.D., Byzantine Christians may well have comprised a majority of the population in Iraq.[1] Also, because of shifting populations and immigrations into Mesopotamia during these years, by the sixth century A.D., not much was left of the original Babylonian population. The ethnic descendants of the early Mesopotamian inhabitants (Babylonians, Assyrians, etc.) had been both decimated by and absorbed into the many waves of invaders and settlers.

The Arabs and Baghdad's World Empire

The nations and peoples discussed above were not Arab. The Arabs originally inhabited the area in and around the Arabian Peninsula, the general area that is now Saudi Arabia and Yemen. At the end of the sixth century A.D., Mohammed converted the pagan Arabian tribes to his new monotheistic religion Islam and united them into a powerful military force. The Arabs began expanding and conquering numerous regions, both to the north (Mesopotamia) and to the west (North Africa). By the early seventh century A.D., the Arabs were fighting against the Sassanid Iranians in Iraq. Weakened by years of fighting with the Byzantines and not overly popular with the local population in Mesopotamia, the Sassanids were no match for the Arabian armies. By A.D. 636, the Arabs had driven the Persian Sassanids out of Iraq and back into Persia. Soon, however, the Islamic faith would spread to Persia and would become the dominant religion there as well.[2]

During these years, thousands of Bedouin Arabs emigrated to Iraq and settled in the region between the Tigris and Euphrates Rivers that had once been known as Babylonia. Although most of the existing population at that time was Christian, the church there was primarily Byzantine and was associated with the weak Byzantine Empire, which was rife with theological and territorial disputes and divisions. The Byzantine armies were quickly driven back toward Constantinople (Byzantium, modern-day Istanbul) in western Turkey. Already weakened by theological division and incessant infighting among themselves, the Christians in Iraq, with a few exceptions noted below, capitulated to Islam within a few generations, intermarrying with the new Arab inhabitants and adopting their religious beliefs.

Shortly after the Arabs conquered the region now known as Iraq, the Islamic faith suffered a tumultuous schism. Theological differences turned into open war, precipitated by a struggle over succession to the top leadership position (the caliphate) of the new Arab Empire. Ali Bin Abi Taleb, Mohammad's cousin and son-in-law, challenged the lax piety of the ruling powers, criticized them for not following the Koran correctly, and then tried to take power in order to purify the faith.

After an extended struggle and numerous battles, Ali was assassinated (A.D. 661). However, the theological rift between the two warring groups was never healed. The group that followed Ali, composed of Arabs who had emigrated to Iraq and Persia, became known as the Shias, while the other theological party in Islam became known as the Sunnis. These two groups, Shia and Sunni, still exist today, and the tensions between them are as deep-seated as those between Protestants and Catholics in Northern Ireland.

Meanwhile, control of the vast new Arab Empire was consolidated by the Umayyad dynasty. They established their capital in Damascus and ruled over the Arab world from A.D. 661 to A.D. 750. However, in A.D. 750, a new dynasty (Abbasid) wrested control of Iraq and Iran from the Umayyads and then quickly gained control of the entire Arab Empire. They moved the capital of the empire to Baghdad in Iraq and reigned from A.D. 750 to A.D. 1258.

Ali Babba and the Golden Era of Arab Civilization

The Abbasid dynasty controlled a huge empire and ushered in what has often been called the "golden era of Arab civilization." In the late eighth century A.D., the Abbasid caliphate ruled an empire that stretched from Spain to the border of India, encompassing North Africa, Egypt, Arabia, Palestine, Syria, Mesopotamia, and Iran. At the center of this empire was the spectacular capital city of Baghdad. Without doubt, during the early years of the Abbasid dynasty, Baghdad was the most powerful city in the world.

The economy of Iraq boomed during this time. The irrigation systems of the ancient Mesopotamians were rebuilt and improved, and agriculture once again flourished. Likewise Arab traders transported goods from all over the known world, and many of the major trade routes ran once again through Iraq. The population flourished and grew rapidly. Population estimates for Iraq during this time period run as high as twenty-nine million people.[3] Arab intellectual life also flourished, and the Arabs led the world in many areas of science, philosophy, art, and literature. It was during this time that the famous book *Arabian Nights* was written.

The Abbasid Arab Empire, centered in Baghdad and stretching from India to Spain, far surpassed anything King Nebuchadnezzar of Babylon ever dreamed of. As far as significant empires go, this one can be rivaled only by ancient Rome. Naturally, Saddam Hussein has claimed a connection between his reign and that of the Abbasids. In reality, this claim is more accurate than claims of a Babylonian connection, and certainly the Iraqi people should take great pride in their Arab heritage of this era. The builders of the extensive empire under the Abbasid dynasty were Arabs, many of them from the same Bedouin tribes that had emigrated to Iraq. Many of the current residents of Iraq are descendents of these same Arab tribes.

Mongols and Turks

Of course, empires do not last forever, and the Abbasid dynasty soon began losing control of some of its territories (Spain, Egypt, Iran). The continued strife between the Sunni and Shia factions within the Islamic empire also took its toll. After the Arab Empire had grown relatively weak, in A.D. 1258, an army of Mongols swept into the area from northeastern Asia and devastated the entire region of Iraq. Unlike earlier invaders such as the Arabs, the Mongols did not immigrate and did not build cities and cultures. They simply destroyed everything. Upon capturing Baghdad, one of the intellectual centers of the world at the time, the Mongols executed all the scholars and poets in the city and then destroyed it. Throughout the country they destroyed the elaborate irrigation systems, thus eliminating the agricultural basis for the large population. Chaos ensued, and the economy collapsed. The sophisticated urban intellectual cities of the Abbasids disappeared, and the people who survived lapsed into subsistence pastoralism. Iraq slid back into the dark ages.

In the centuries that followed the disastrous Mongol invasion, Iraq found herself helplessly caught between the more powerful regimes in Iran to the east and Turkey to the west. Indeed, the Iranians and the Ottoman Turks fought over Iraq, and both groups invaded several times. Eventually, the Ottomans won, but the devastated prize was not worth much. Under the reign of the Ottomans, by the mid-1800s, the squalid population in Iraq had shrunk to less than 1.5 million.[4]

Much of the fighting during this time was related to the long-standing Sunni-Shia schism within Islam. The Iranians, predominately Shia Muslims, appealed to the Shia Muslims in Iraq to assist them in fighting the Ottomans. Likewise, the Ottomans, predominately Sunni Muslims, called on the Sunnis in Iraq to ally with them against Iran. Because the Ottomans ultimately won out and ruled Iraq for over two hundred years, Sunni Muslims in Iraq came to dominate most local governments and practically all the military officer corps.

The heritage of this conflict still plagues Iraq to this day, and it has influenced many of Saddam Hussein's political and military actions. If Saddam's regime falls, these long-standing rivalries and religious factions are likely to resurface in violent fashion.

Oil and British Control

Shortly after the dawn of the twentieth century, oil was discovered in Iran. As Britain began operating rich Iranian oil fields, a new dimension was added to the complexity of the Middle East. When World War I broke out, the Ottoman Turks, who controlled Iraq, aligned themselves with Germany against Britain and France. Fearful of losing the Iranian oil fields, the British landed an army from India in southern Iraq and marched on Baghdad. The British also allied themselves with several Arab tribes of Arabia and sought to drive the Ottoman Turks out of Arabia, Palestine, and Syria (you may recall the portrayal of this event in the famous movie *Lawrence of Arabia*). The Arabs assisting the British had been led to believe that after driving out the Turks a large, independent Arab state would be created, one that included the Arabian Peninsula, Palestine, Syria, Lebanon, and Mesopotamia (Iraq).[5]

THE BRITISH-INSTALLED MONARCHY

However, the possibility of a large, independent Arab state vanished in the aftermath of World War I as the European victors divided the Middle East into areas of control (mandates) under Britain and France. Decisions were made based on what was in the best interest of Britain and France, not what was best for the Arabs or the other inhabitants of the area. Britain was given control of Mesopotamia, along with Egypt, Arabia, and Palestine. Syria and Lebanon went to the French. In 1919, European mapmakers at a conference in Paris drew the boundaries for the newly created countries within the British and French mandates. The modern country of Iraq, both its name and its current borders, were created at this conference. Little attention was given to ethnic, linguistic, or religious groupings in Mesopotamia as the international map lines were drawn. Rather, Britain was largely concerned with its own economic and political interests (primarily related to oil) and with keeping the new entities at manageable levels of power. Shia Muslims and Sunni Muslims were both included in the new country of Iraq, as was a large population of Kurds, a group unrelated ethnically to either the Arabs of Iraq or the Persian Iranians.

To govern this new country (under close British control), the British established a new monarchy, something unknown in Iraq for centuries. They chose, not someone from Iraq, but Faisal, the son of the Sharif of Mecca, to be the new king of Iraq. He had been one of Britain's key allies in the Arabian-British campaign to push the Turks out of Arabia, Palestine, and Syria.

Of course, such a monarchy was doomed from the beginning. The Iraqis viewed Faisal as an outsider, for he had never lived in Iraq. Indeed, he had never even been to Iraq before being crowned king.[6] Furthermore, the British were afraid to help him develop a strong government. It was in their interest to keep him ineffectual and thus dependant on British military support. Both the British and the new king continued the Ottoman practice of using primarily Sunni Muslims to staff government positions and the army officer corps, even though the Shia Muslims now comprised a majority of the population in Iraq.[7]

THE IRAQI REPUBLIC

During the 1930s and 1940s, Iraqi politics were characterized by both national and pan-Arab movements. The monarchy, viewed as a puppet of Britain, became increasingly unpopular. In 1941, with World War II well under way, the military overthrew the monarchy. Worried that the new Iraqi regime might side with the Germans, Britain responded by landing an army, capturing Baghdad, and reinstating the monarchy.

In the years following World War II, the British "Empire" was dismantled, and direct British influence in Middle Eastern affairs began to wane slightly. In 1958, the monarchy in Iraq was once again overthrown by a military coup, and this time the British did not intervene. Leading the coup, and the one to emerge as the new leader of Iraq, was a general named Abd al Karim Qasim.

Saddam and the Baath Party

During the 1940s and 1950s, a political party called the Baath Party slowly grew in power and influence. Vehemently opposed to a monarchy, the party was also opposed to Qasim. In fact, in 1959, several Baath members attempted unsuccessfully to assassinate General Qasim. One of the unsuccessful assassins was a twenty-two-year-old Arab named Saddam Hussein, who was wounded in the attack. The injured Saddam fled to Egypt, where he stayed for several years until things calmed down in Iraq.

In 1963, the Baath Party, probably with CIA support and encouragement, overthrew the military rulers of Iraq.[8] However, within a year, another group of military officers had regained power. Yet the Baath Party continued to grow stronger and to organize more effectively, and in 1968, they staged another coup and took back control of Iraq. Many of the key leaders in the Baath Party at this critical time were Sunni Arabs from the northwest town of Tikrit. The top leader was Ahmad Hasan al Bakr, and his right-hand man was Saddam Hussein.

Over the next ten years, Bakr's health began to fail, and Saddam began to consolidate for himself more and more of the political and military power. Eventually, Bakr realized this, and in 1979 he resigned. Saddam Hussein replaced him and became president of the republic, leader of the Baath Party, and commander in chief of the armed forces.[9]

The Iraqi Patchwork Quilt of Religions and Ethnicities

The tumultuous history of Iraq has resulted in a patchwork quilt of religions and ethnicities. Approximately 76 percent of the population is ethnic Arab. These Arabs speak Arabic and embrace Arab culture. The Kurds, a non-Arabic people, comprise 19 percent of the population and have never really considered themselves Iraqis.

They desire their own country and throughout the twentieth century frequently fought against the Arab majority. The other 5 percent is composed of several ethnic minorities: Muslim Turkomans, Christian Assyrians, and Christian Armenians. There is still a smattering of Iranians, but most of them were expelled and sent to Iran in the 1970s. The Christian Assyrians, comprising less than 1 percent of the population, are the only ones who can claim an ethnic connection to ancient Babylon. They still speak Aramaic and probably are the direct (more or less) descendants of the Babylonians.

There are very few Jews in Iraq. Although for much of Iraq's history there was a fairly large and prosperous Jewish community in Baghdad, almost all the Jews fled between 1948 and 1952.

As discussed earlier, one of the deepest and most significant divisions in Iraq is between the Sunni Muslims and the Shia Muslims. The Shia Arabs make up the majority of the population. Estimates (which are politically charged) range from 55 to 65 percent. The Kurds are Sunni Muslims, but they have a historical animosity for all Arabs in the country, Sunni or otherwise. The Sunni Arabs, who historically have dominated the religious, political, and military power base of the country, actually make up only roughly 13 percent of the population.[10] Iraq has been and continues to be an ethnic powder keg that is ready to blow wide open as soon as the strong-armed power of the ruling tyrant is removed.

Christians in Iraq

Surprisingly, approximately 3 percent of Iraq's population is Christian, at least in name. Although some missionary work took root in Iraq in the twentieth century (especially by the Presbyterians), the majority of the Christians in Iraq are from ethnic groups that have been "Christian" since the fourth or fifth century A.D. (Many of these people are Christian in name only. The beliefs of many of these groups differ from those of mainstream American evangelicalism, and, in fact, most evangelicals in America today would have doubts as to whether many of these people are truly saved.)

Even more surprising is the fact that Tariq Aziz, one of the highest-ranking officials in Saddam Hussein's government and perhaps the most visible Iraqi spokesman to the West, comes from one of these Christian groups. He belongs to the Chaldean Christian Church, a group of Christians in the East who remained loyal to Rome when most of the Eastern churches switched their allegiance to Constantinople (Byzantium). There are about ten thousand Chaldean Christians in Baghdad. Richard Butler, former leader of the UNSCOM weapons inspection teams in Iraq, shares many of his frustrating encounters with Aziz in his recent book *The Greatest Threat*. Butler suggests that Aziz is able to assume such a high position in Saddam's government precisely because he comes from a non-Muslim ethnic group and thus cannot pose a power threat to Saddam himself.[11]

As mentioned above, the Assyrian Christians make up one of the larger Christian minority groups, although they comprise less than 1 percent of the Iraqi population. It is interesting and somewhat ironic that this particular group is the only one that has a clear ethnic connection to the ancient Babylonians. In other words, the only real Babylonians in the world today are Christians, at least in name.

Conclusion

One of the things that stands out from this discussion is that Saddam Hussein is an Arab and not a Babylonian. In fact, he has no ethnic connection to the ancient Babylonians. Furthermore, most of the Iraqi people have no connection to the Babylonians other than that they occupy the same piece of terrain. Sandra Mackey stresses this in her book *The Reckoning: Iraq and the Legacy of Saddam Hussein*. She writes, "Few Iraqis see themselves as descendants of the Mesopotamians for the most basic and simple of reasons—their ancestors never lived in the land between the rivers." Mackey quotes an Arab scholar who states, "Visions of Mesopotamia are not important to Iraqis. It is nothing but official discourse. For the people, Mesopotamia is a dead issue."[12]

A similar situation could be found at the present time in New York City. If we were to walk around New York City today, we would observe a large number of ethnic groups. How many of them, do you suppose, feel connected to the original Indians who lived in Manhattan when the first European ship arrived? A reconstructed Indian village in New York City would be interesting historically but hardly a sign that something important was happening politically, and the current inhabitants of New York City would not feel any emotional attachment to the village.

The move by Saddam Hussein to rebuild Babylon does not strike a chord in the hearts of the Iraqi people, and his comparison of himself to King Nebuchadnezzar likewise rings hollow for most of his people. Even for Saddam, the rebuilt Babylon is probably no more than a historical monument, a tourist attraction, and an attempt to rally national pride and to unite his people. It is currently much closer to a theme park than to the center of a world government. It is certainly presented this way on Iraq's tourist web site. And in all probability, if and when Saddam is removed, the Babylon project will recede into the background and will become merely another interesting reconstructed site to be visited by archaeologists, tourists, and local school children. It seems unlikely that it signals the beginning of the end-times.

NINE

Are We Entering the End-Times?

■

In *Are We Living in the End Times?* the prophecy book that follows the Left Behind series of novels, Tim LaHaye and Jerry Jenkins argue that we are indeed entering the end-times. They base this view in part on the reconstruction of ancient Babylon by Saddam Hussein. Charles Dyer argues for the same basic point in *The Rise of Babylon: Sign of the End Times.* One of the goals of the present book has been to analyze that claim from both a biblical and a historical basis.

The Truth of the Bible

The Bible is true and without error, and therefore Christians should study the Scriptures carefully and honestly, searching for the meaning the authors (divine and human) of the Bible intended to communicate. Christians should also seek to know what God has revealed about the future.

Yet Christians today are only students of biblical prophecy; we are not prophets. Our goal, therefore, should be to find the meaning the prophets placed in the Bible, not to create a new meaning. The Word of God is true and powerful, and it does not need us to try to buttress it with clever schemes that supposedly prove that biblical prophecy is indeed coming true before our eyes. God's prophetic word will come true; he does not need us to skew the current geopolitical reality in the world to try to establish a peculiar understanding of his Word. Furthermore, God has some pretty strong words of warning against confusing our prophecies with his and proclaiming our misunderstanding of his Word dogmatically as "thus saith the Lord."

A Place for Christian Humility?

The dogmatic certainty that many writers project when proclaiming their understanding of biblical prophecy, especially their view that the end-times are upon us, is distressing. There are many beliefs about which Christians should be certain and dogmatic (the love of God; the death, resurrection, and return of Christ; etc.). However, when it comes to end-time prophecy, Bible-believing Christians hold to a wide range of views. Should we each take the attitude that everybody is wrong but me? Or should we formulate our views and state them in such a way that shows we acknowledge and respect views that differ from ours but are still based on the Bible? What we need is a little more Christian humility in this field of study.

Another phenomenon that is of concern is that many (if not most) Bible-believing scholars—those who read Greek and Hebrew, have spent their lives studying and teaching the Word of God, and have written scholarly commentaries and theologies—frequently arrive at understandings of the Bible that differ from those of writers who influence popular views of prophecy in the church today. If a popular writer finds out that a majority of evangelical, Bible-believing scholars disagrees with his view because of biblical evidence, perhaps that writer should tone down his assertion of absolute certainty and acknowledge the possible validity of the other view.

Furthermore, throughout the history of the Christian church, writers and preachers have tended to view the end-time prophecies of the Bible in light of their particular times and places in history. For example, because the Protestant Reformers of the sixteenth century were struggling against Roman Catholicism, they read their struggle into their biblical understanding of the end-time prophecies and thus proclaimed the pope as the Antichrist and Catholicism as the evil world empire striving to destroy God's people. In the 1940s, Adolf Hitler was the Antichrist. In the 1970s, we feared the Soviet Union, and therefore the Soviets became the bad guys of Revelation. Now, suddenly, Muslims are the bad guys. Christians should be suspicious of this remarkable coincidence and with humility see this approach to the Bible as egocentric. We must guard against the natural tendency to think that God's plan for the ages revolves

around *our* generation and will naturally come to frui-
tion during *our* lifetime.

The Fall of Babylon: Once Is Enough

The evidence presented throughout this book reveals
that the Bible does not predict the rise of Babylon in
the end-times. As demonstrated, the prophecies of Isaiah and Jeremiah concerning the fall of Babylon were
fulfilled long ago in history. Thus, there is no prophetic
need to rebuild Babylon just so it can be destroyed a
second time, more accurately this time and according
to prophecy. It has already been destroyed according to
prophecy. Saddam Hussein's reconstruction program
for the ancient city of Babylon is no different from other
reconstructions of historical and archaeological sites.
Furthermore, Saddam will probably soon pass from
the scene, and the popular interest in his Babylon park
will no doubt fade. In all probability, the site will then
attract only the same attention that the sites of ancient
Nineveh or ancient Thebes attract. It is doubtful that
the archaeological site at Babylon will become the
capital of a world government, the functioning center
of world commerce and political power, as doomsday
writers predict.

Arabs and Babylonians

Historical background is also important for us as
Christians to study. Familiarity with the fascinating (but
violent) history of Iraq can help us understand the complex situation in that region of the world. As shown, Sad-

dam Hussein and most of the Iraqis are not related to the ancient Babylonians. Saddam's Arab ancestors did not enter Mesopotamia until the seventh century A.D., and the majority of the Iraqi population is Arab, not Babylonian. Indeed, they have very little ethnic, historical, or cultural connection to the ancient Babylonians. Ironically, the only direct descendants of the Babylonians in Iraq today are Assyrian Christians.

Rome—Past and Future

Another point of disagreement between the conclusions of this book and those of many popular prophecy writers concerns Rome and the Roman Empire. There is no clear evidence that a revived Roman Empire will appear in the end-times. Furthermore, there is not much similarity between the modern fifteen-member (soon to be twenty-five-member) European Union and the ten-horned beast of Daniel, which supposedly represents a revived ancient Roman Empire. To equate the Roman Empire (which included North Africa) with modern Europe (Poland, Finland, Sweden, etc.) is historically and geographically inaccurate.

On the other hand, Rome does play an important role in understanding the Book of Revelation. Strong evidence indicates that the harlot who sits on seven hills in Revelation 17 and 18 probably represents ancient Rome, not a future rebuilt city of Babylon. Starting in the Old Testament and carrying over into the New Testament, the term *Babylon* was often used as a symbol for evil and hostility toward God's people. John uses the term in this fashion in the Book of Revelation.

How Should Christians Respond to Saddam and Iraq?

How, then, should Christians respond to Saddam Hussein and his activities in Iraq? First of all, it is important for American Christians to view themselves as part of the universal church, the worldwide body of Christ. The body of Christ is a vast, international body, not an American institution. It is quite tempting and rather easy for American Christians to equate America with the biblical people of God and thus to assume without reflection that the current enemies of America are the biblical enemies of God. As mentioned above, isn't it a coincidence that in the 1970s and 1980s popular prophecy writers saw the Soviet Union as the biblical end-time invader, and now, as America struggles with radical Islamic terrorists, these same prophecy writers have identified Muslims as the end-time enemy?

Don't misunderstand. The Western media have not exaggerated the extent of Saddam Hussein's evil character. He is a heartless, cold-blooded killer, one who well epitomizes the meaning of evil. Yet evil has been with us for some time now, and Saddam's evil character does not automatically qualify him as the one to fulfill biblical prophecy in the end-times.

Also, as evil as Saddam Hussein is, we as Christians must be careful that we do not fire our shotgun of prophetic "Christian" judgment blindly into the international community. For example, is it right for us to accuse Ethiopia—as Tim LaHaye and Jerry Jenkins do—of currently scheming to rebel against God and invade Israel as part of an evil Russian-led coalition? As part of the body of Christ, should we not feel the bond of Christian brotherhood with the faithful believers in Ethiopia, in Russia, and even in Iraq? How do you suppose the Christian doomsday books affect Christian mission work in Muslim lands? It is difficult to lead people to the Lord when they feel that Christians have vilified them and have stereotyped them as evil.

Christians believe in the second coming of Christ, and we wait expectantly for that glorious event. However, for years prophecy "experts" have been saying that the end is just around the corner. LaHaye proclaims that it will come in five, ten, or at the most twenty years. Of course, Christians should give proper attention to biblical prophecy, but an overemphasis on the imminent end and the accompanying consequential hopelessness of the world situation does not serve the cause of Christ. The current fixation of many American Christians on the prediction that a hopeless world situation must precede the end-times leads them to assume that the world situation is indeed hopeless. This doom-and-gloom attitude often causes Christians to withdraw into little pessimistic groups and to lose interest in the evangelism and social action that our Lord has called us to. Jesus never called us to doom-and-gloom pessimism.

However, many Christians in America have indeed fallen into viewing the future as only doom and gloom, and much of the current popular end-time prophecy literature feeds this tendency. Yet the message of the Bible is one of hope. The gospel is spreading like wildfire across Africa and Latin America. Missionaries and nationals are proclaiming the gospel in Russia and China, and in former Soviet-controlled countries such as Romania, the church is blossoming and growing by leaps and bounds. Should we respond to this with hopeless despair? No! Let's send more missionaries to Russia. Let's evangelize the Russians with hope and optimism instead of pronouncing them evil and projecting them into questionable end-time scenarios. Many Christian mission agencies and individual churches have begun to focus their attention on Muslim countries. Our energies would be much better spent supporting their efforts to reach the Muslim world for Christ than trying to prove with questionable evidence that these Muslims are part of an evil end-time coalition intent on defying God.

In conclusion, therefore, Saddam Hussein's reconstruction of ancient Babylon has nothing to do with end-time biblical prophecy. Likewise, the likelihood of an imminent Russian-led Muslim invasion of Israel is doubtful, as is the connection between the European Union and a revived Roman Empire. These positions are not biblical. What is biblical is focusing our energy on the spread and strengthening of the church. What is biblical is Jesus' command to go and make disciples of all nations.

A world government is not coming to Babylon, and a Russian-led Muslim invasion of Israel is not about to take place. What is very probable is that the United States may find herself in the very near future burdened with the difficult and costly task of replacing Saddam Hussein's evil regime and trying to restore peace, order, and sanity to the millions of people in that troubled country. We as Christians should approach this difficult task with grace, the love of Christ, and the gospel, along with some solid socioeconomic and medical help, rather than with end-time charts and conspiracy theories.

Notes

![icon]

Chapter 1

1. Actually, as discussed in chapter 5, Hal Lindsey still maintains that the Russians will be involved in this invasion, but he now argues that the Muslims will comprise a large portion of the army.

2. The basic conversation and the general tenor of this story are true. The names and some of the details have been changed.

3. Tim F. LaHaye and Jerry B. Jenkins, *Left Behind: A Novel of the Earth's Last Days* (Carol Stream, Ill.: Tyndale, 1995).

4. Hal Lindsey spearheads this approach; see his earliest work, with C. C. Carlson, *The Late Great Planet Earth* (Grand Rapids: Zondervan, 1970), 48. Other authors in this vein of thought include Grant R. Jeffrey, *Armageddon: Appointment with Destiny* (Toronto: Frontier Research, 1988); Chuck Smith, *Future Survival* (Costa Mesa, Calif.: Calvary Chapel, 1978); Edgar C. Whisenant, *88 Reasons Why the Rapture Will Be in 1988* (Nashville: World Bible Society, 1988); Wesley Meacham, *Troubled Waters: Prophecy from a Layman's Point of View* (New York: Vantage, 1988); and David Reagan, *The Master Plan: Making Sense of the Controversies Surrounding Bible Prophecy Today* (Eugene, Ore.: Harvest House, 1993).

5. Charles H. Dyer, *World News and Bible Prophecy* (Wheaton: Tyndale, 1995), 166–75. Hal Lindsey's first book, *The Late Great Planet Earth*, claimed that the Soviet Union would invade Israel in the end-times. But in later works, Lindsey switched to the view that the end-time invasion of Israel would be Muslim in nature and led by Iran. See *Planet Earth—2000 A.D.: Will Mankind Survive?* (Palos Verdes, Calif.: Western Front, 1994), 169–202; and his latest book, *The Everlasting Hatred: The Roots of Jihad* (Murrieta, Calif.: Oracle House Publishing, 2002), 233–35.

6. Charles H. Dyer, *The Rise of Babylon: Sign of the End Times* (Wheaton: Tyndale, 1991), 191–202; and idem, *World News and Bible Prophecy*, 181–239.

Chapter 2

1. Saïd K. Aburish, *Saddam Hussein: The Politics of Revenge* (London: Bloomsbury, 2001), 127.

2. Charles H. Dyer, *The Rise of Babylon: Sign of the End Times* (Wheaton: Tyndale, 1991).

3. "Permanently Powerful?" *Newsweek* (16 March 1998): 41.

4. Rick MacInnes-Rae, "Saddam's Babylon," CBC Radio, August 2002, reprinted at cbc.ca/news/features/iraq/correspondents/macinnesrae.html.

5. Walter R. Bodine, "The Sumerians," in *Peoples of the Old Testament World*, ed. A. J. Hoerth, G. L. Mattingly, and E. M. Yamauchi (Grand Rapids: Baker; Cambridge: Lutterworth Press, 1994), 19–42.

6. Sandra Mackey, *The Reckoning: Iraq and the Legacy of Saddam Hussein* (New York: W. W. Norton, 2002), 239.

7. For a good discussion on Hammurabi and his law code, see Jack M. Sasson, "King Hammurabi of Babylon," in *Civilizations of the Ancient Near East*, ed. Jack M. Sasson (Peabody, Mass.: Hendrickson, 2000), 901–15.

8. Mackey, *Reckoning*, 252.

9. Aburish, *Saddam Hussein*, chronicles Saddam's attempt to unite the Arab world with him as its leader. See especially 115–18, 254–58.

10. Ibid., 127.

11. Ibid., 176. Aburish argues throughout his book that Saddam's real model, the leader he actually followed in action rather than just in public propaganda, was Joseph Stalin.

12. Ibid., 201–2.

Chapter 3

1. Old Testament scholars acknowledge that Genesis 10 is notoriously difficult to interpret with certainty. For example, the cities identified as centers of Nimrod's kingdom (Gen. 10:10–11) are all located in Mesopotamia. Yet in 10:8, Nimrod's father is identified as Cush. Cush is a country located south of Egypt, and the connection to Mesopotamia is not clear. Also, scholars have noted that the genealogy of Genesis 10 contains the names not only of people but also of tribes, countries, and cities. Furthermore, many scholars have observed that genealogies in the ancient world were often used to present alliances and geopolitical associations in addition to physical descent. For a detailed discussion of some of the problems and a proposed solution, see J. Daniel Hays, *From Every People and Nation: A Biblical Theology of Race* (Downers Grove, Ill.: InterVarsity, 2003), chap. 3.

2. Shinar was in Mesopotamia, a territory that was first called Sumer, then Sumer and Akkad, and then Babylonia. In fact, Shinar probably comes from the word *Sumer;* see Victor P. Hamilton, *The Book of Genesis Chapters*

1–17, New International Commentary on the Old Testament (Grand Rapids: Eerdmans, 1990), 351.

3. For a picture of the site taken in 1902 that demonstrates the totally desolated look of the city, see Joan Oates, *Babylon*, rev. ed. (London: Thames & Hudson, 1986), 145.

4. Ibid., 136–43.

Chapter 4

1. Charles H. Dyer, *World News and Bible Prophecy* (Wheaton: Tyndale, 1995), 154–55.

2. Tim LaHaye, "Foreword," in Joseph Chambers, *A Palace for the Antichrist: Saddam Hussein's Drive to Rebuild Babylon and Its Place in Bible Prophecy* (Green Forest, Ark.: New Leaf Press, 1996), 12–13.

3. Ibid., 26.

4. See Charles H. Dyer, *The Rise of Babylon: Sign of the End Times* (Wheaton: Tyndale, 1991), 19.

5. Ibid., 163–65.

6. This is the view of John N. Oswalt, *Isaiah*, New International Commentary on the Old Testament (Grand Rapids: Eerdmans, 1998), 277; Geoffrey W. Grogan, "Isaiah," in *The Expositor's Bible Commentary*, ed. Frank E. Gaebelein (Grand Rapids: Zondervan, 1986), 281; John Goldingay, *Isaiah*, New International Biblical Commentary (Peabody, Mass.: Hendrickson, 2001), 276; Brevard Childs, *Isaiah*, Old Testament Library (Louisville: Westminster John Knox, 2001), 376; John Calvin, *Isaiah*, Calvin's Commentaries (Grand Rapids: AP&A, n.d.), 665, Page H. Kelley, "Isaiah," in *The Broadman Bible Commentary*, ed. Clifton J. Allen (Nashville: Broadman, 1971), 327; John A. Martin, "Isaiah," in *The Bible Knowledge Commentary, Old Testament*, ed. John F. Walvoord and Roy B. Zuck (Wheaton: Victor Books, 1985), 1102; Herbert M. Wolf, *Interpreting Isaiah* (Grand Rapids: Zondervan, 1985), 203–4; J. Alec Motyer, *Isaiah*, Tyndale Old Testament Commentaries (Downers Grove, Ill.: InterVarsity, 1999), 304; and many others. This view is also taken by Charles Ryrie in the Ryrie Study Bible and likewise by the editors of the NIV Study Bible.

7. Edwin M. Yamauchi, *Persia and the Bible* (Grand Rapids: Baker, 1990), 54–57.

8. Surprisingly, Dyer himself acknowledges this. He writes, "In the Old Testament, 'the day of the Lord' originally referred to any time God entered history to settle accounts with humankind." However, Dyer then goes on to argue that the meaning later *developed* to refer to only the coming judgment on all the world and Israel in the end-times (*Rise of Babylon*, 163–64). Is Dyer suggesting that the prophecies of Isaiah were composed or written down late in Israel's history after the meaning had changed? Or is he suggesting that Isaiah the prophet (who preaches fairly early) meant it to refer to judgment in general when he proclaimed it but that the actual meaning of his prophecy later changed? If so, who changed it?

9. Tim LaHaye and Jerry Jenkins, *Are We Living in the End Times?* (Wheaton: Tyndale, 1999), 137.

Chapter 5

1. Iain M. Duguid, *Ezekiel*, The NIV Application Commentary (Grand Rapids: Zondervan, 1999), 452.

2. Tim LaHaye and Jerry Jenkins, *Are We Living in the End Times?* (Wheaton: Tyndale, 1999), 85.

3. Ibid., 86–87.

4. Ibid., 92.

5. It is uncertain whom LaHaye and Jenkins are referring to when they say "prophecy scholars." The Evangelical Theological Society, for example, is one of the largest and most significant organizations in which biblical scholars from seminaries, Bible colleges, and Christian universities come together to study and discuss the Bible. Among the members who teach and write in the area of Old Testament and Old Testament prophecy, we do not know of *anyone* who holds this view of Ezekiel. On the contrary, the top evangelical experts on the Book of Ezekiel specifically denounce this view. See, for example, Daniel I. Block, *The Book of Ezekiel: Chapters 25–48*, New International Commentary on the Old Testament (Grand Rapids: Eerdmans, 1998), 434; and Duguid, *Ezekiel*, 453.

6. For an up-to-date listing of oil producers, see the web site "Oil and Gas International: Your Online Prime Source for Worldwide E&P News, Information, and Analysis" at www.oilandgasinternational.com.

7. This section is dependent on C. Marvin Pate and Calvin B. Haines, *Doomsday Delusions: What's Wrong with Predictions about the End of the World* (Downers Grove, Ill.: InterVarsity, 1995), 61–63.

8. LaHaye and Jenkins, *Are We Living in the End Times?* 89–90.

9. Barry Beitzel, *The Moody Atlas of Bible Lands* (Chicago: Moody, 1985), 4.

10. Edwin Yamauchi, *Foes from the Northern Frontier* (Grand Rapids: Baker, 1982), 19–27.

11. Block, *Ezekiel*, 434.

12. Duguid, *Ezekiel*, 453.

13. Yamauchi, *Foes from the Northern Frontier*, 22–24. Perhaps the leading theory is that *Gog* refers to the famous king of Lydia, "Gyges," and that *Magog* refers to the "land of Gyges," but there is no consensus among scholars about this identification. See Yamauchi, *Foes from the Northern Frontier*, 19–28.

14. Ibid., 24–27. The testimony consists of the Assyrian texts (Tiglath-Pileser I [1115–1077 B.C.], Ashurnasirpal II [883–859 B.C.], Sargon II [721–705 B.C.], Herodotus [c. fourth century B.C. 7.72]; Josephus [c. A.D. 90, *Antiquities of the Jews* 1.124]).

15. For the following, see Pate and Haines, *Doomsday Delusions*, 135–38.

16. Paul Boyer, *When Time Shall Be No More: Prophecy Beliefs in Modern American Culture* (Cambridge: Harvard University Press, 1992), 325–31.

17. Hal Lindsey, *Planet Earth—2000 A.D.: Will Mankind Survive?* (Palos Verdes, Calif.: Western Front, 1994), 169–202.

18. LaHaye and Jenkins, *Are We Living in the End Times?* 94.

19. Ibid. See Hal Lindsey with C. C. Carlson, *The Late Great Planet Earth* (Grand Rapids: Zondervan, 1970), 67–68, 146–68.

20. Lindsey, *Late Great Planet Earth*, 191–96.

21. Ibid., 190–91.

22. Block, *Ezekiel*, 436.

23. Duguid, *Ezekiel*, 453–54.

Chapter 6

1. Charles H. Dyer, *World News and Bible Prophecy* (Wheaton: Tyndale, 1995), 206.

2. For a map of the limits of the Roman Empire in the first century A.D., see James S. Jeffers, *The Greco-Roman World of the New Testament Era* (Downers Grove, Ill.: InterVarsity, 1999), 329.

3. Tim LaHaye and Jerry Jenkins, *Are We Living in the End Times?* (Wheaton: Tyndale, 1999), 169. They even give a timetable for this occurrence: "We are convinced that unless God intervenes, the one-worlders will not give up until they make the United Nations the ruling force of the world by at least 2025—and maybe sooner!" (170).

4. Consider the breakup of the Soviet Union into numerous smaller countries. Likewise, Yugoslavia has split into several ethnic-oriented government entities. In numerous countries of the world, various groups and subgroups are clamoring for independence from larger regional governmental control. The Kurds in Iraq and in Turkey are a prime example. Several African countries and a few Asian countries are struggling with this phenomenon as well.

5. Israel's sin is personified by a woman in Zechariah's vision because the Hebrew word for wickedness is feminine in gender. There is no implied connection between women in general and iniquity, for the two women with wings play a positive role in the story when they carry the basket to Babylonia.

6. See the discussion by Carol L. Meyers and Eric M. Meyers, *Haggai-Zechariah 1–8*, Anchor Bible (Garden City, N.Y.: Doubleday, 1987), 294–316.

7. This is the thesis of Saïd K. Aburish in *Saddam Hussein: The Politics of Revenge* (London: Bloomsbury, 2001).

Chapter 7

1. Reported in Scott Lindlaw, "Cheney Presses Need to Bring Down Saddam," *Arkansas Democrat Gazette*, 9 September 2002, p. 1A.

2. Charles H. Dyer, *The Rise of Babylon: Sign of the End Times* (Wheaton: Tyndale, 1991), 23.

3. The quotes that follow are typical of those Dyer seized upon as proof that Babylon is rising again, thus signaling the end-times (ibid., 13–46).

4. John Burns, "New Babylon Is Stalled by a Modern Upheaval," *New York Times International*, 11 October 1990, p. A13.

5. Paul Lewis, "Nebuchadnezzer's Revenge: Iraq Flexes Its Muscles by Rebuilding Babylon," *San Francisco Chronicle*, 30 April 1989, quoted in Dyer, *Rise of Babylon*, 25.

6. *Baghdad Observer*, 23 September 1987, p. 2, quoted in ibid., 42.

7. Amitzai Baram (Hafia University), *Newsweek* (13 August 1990): 23.

8. Paul Lewis, "Dollars Can Still Get You Scotch and Waterford Crystal in Baghdad," *New York Times*, 12 May 1991, p. 10.

9. Robert L. Thomas, "A Classical Dispensationalist View," in *Four Views on the Book of Revelation*, ed. C. Marvin Pate (Grand Rapids: Zondervan, 1998), 177–229.

10. For example, see the following Roman sources: Juvenal, *Satires* 9.130; Horace, *Carmen Saeculare* 5; Ovid, *Tristia* 1.5.69; Pliny, *Natural History* 3.66–67.

11. The following discussion comes from David E. Aune, *Revelation 17–22*, Word Biblical Commentary 52c (Nashville: Thomas Nelson, 1998), 919–28.

12. Pliny the Elder, *Natural History* 37-204; LCC translation with modifications. The italicized words indicate the same terms used by Pliny and in Revelation 18:11–13, as noted in Aune, *Revelation 17–22*, 981–82.

13. *Sibylline Oracles* 5.155–70.

14. See the extensive discussion in L. Goppelt, *A Commentary on 1 Peter* (Grand Rapids: Eerdmans, 1993), 373–77; and the good article by E. Randy Richards, "Peter, Babylon, and Rome," *Biblical Illustrator* (summer 1998): 12–15.

15. D. S. Russell, *Apocalyptic: Ancient and Modern* (Philadelphia: Fortress, 1978), 64.

Chapter 8

1. Sandra Mackey, *The Reckoning: Iraq and the Legacy of Saddam Hussein* (New York: W. W. Norton, 2002), 40–41. For a good discussion of the history of Iraq during this period, see Georges Roux, *Ancient Iraq* (New York: Pelican Books, 1977), 370–85.

2. For further reading on the rise of the Arab Empire and its conquest of Mesopotamia, see Philip K. Hitti, *History of the Arabs: From the Earliest Times to the Present* (London: Macmillan, 1964).

3. Helen Chapin Metz, ed., *Iraq: A Country Study*, Federal Research Division (Washington, D.C.: United States Government, 1988), 79.

4. Ibid.

5. Mackey, *Reckoning*, 102–3.

6. Saïd K. Aburish, *Saddam Hussein: The Politics of Revenge* (London: Bloomsbury, 2001), 5.

7. For more reading on this fascinating and important period in Iraqi history, see Charles Tripp, *A History of Iraq* (Cambridge: Cambridge University Press, 2000).

8. Aburish, *Saddam Hussein*, 53–60. The United States was apparently worried about the communist leanings of Qasim.

9. For Saddam's rise to power, see ibid., 38–95; and Tripp, *History of Iraq*, 193–235.

10. Metz, *Iraq*, 79.

11. Richard Butler, *The Greatest Threat: Iraq, Weapons of Mass Destruction, and the Growing Crisis of Global Security* (New York: Public Affairs Books, 2000), 68.

12. Mackey, *Reckoning*, 56.

C. Marvin Pate (M.A., Wheaton College; Ph.D., Marquette University), a pastor for over twenty-five years, also taught in the Bible department at Moody Bible Institute (Chicago) for thirteen years. Pate now teaches Greek, biblical interpretation, and New Testament at Ouachita Baptist University. He is the author or coauthor of eleven books, four of which deal with biblical prophecy: *Doomsday Delusions, The End of the Age Has Come, Four Views of Revelation,* and *The New Testament and the Great Tribulation.* He and his wife, Sherry, live in Arkadelphia, Arkansas.

J. Daniel Hays (Th.M., Dallas Theological Seminary; Ph.D., Southwestern Baptist Theological Seminary), a former missionary to Ethiopia, now teaches Hebrew, biblical interpretation, and Old Testament at Ouachita Baptist University. Hays is the coauthor of *Grasping God's Word: A Hands-On Approach to Reading, Interpreting, and Applying the Bible* and the author of *From Every People and Nation: A Biblical Theology of Race.* He and his wife, Donna, live in Arkadelphia, Arkansas.